Shoji and Kumiko Design

Book 1
The Basics

Shoji and Kumiko Design

Book 1
The Basics

Desmond King

D and M King

ISBN 978-0-9872583-0-4

Photographs by Desmond King and Mariko King

Diagrams by Desmond King

Published by D and M King

Queensland, Australia

kskdesign.com.au

To Mariko and Naomi

CONTENTS

ACKNOWLEDGEMENTS

As I gather my thoughts about the past several months I've spent writing this book, I'd like to acknowledge the many people who have played an instrumental role in my woodworking growth and development.

First I'd like to thank Stuart Bywater of Bywater Design in Brisbane, who taught me what precision in design and in using the hand plane really means.

I owe a major debt of gratitude to all the staff at Shokugei Gakuin. In particular, Board of Directors Chairman Mr. Minoru Inaba and Deputy Principal Sukenari Ikezaki Sensei for giving me the opportunity to realize my dream; Hideo Shimazaki *Tōryō* and Tadao Arai *Tōryō* for steering me in the right direction when needed, and at times confusing me totally with the Toyama-*ben* dialect; furniture instructor Tadashi Kakitani Sensei, whose knowledge and skill was a constant inspiration; Sachio Ueno Sensei, a leading authority on Japanese cultural and architectural history, who encouraged me to explore *kumiko-zaiku*; and Mrs. Shigeko Uetake and all the other members of the admin staff, who made my time at the College as administratively painless as possible.

My deepest gratitude of course goes to my instructor, Isao Sawada Sensei. His expertise, patience and forbearance during my twelve months at Shokugei Gakuin constantly inspired me to expand my goals, and gave me an invaluable understanding of shoji and kumiko, and of the use, maintenance and spirit of Japanese tools. For this, Sawada Sensei, *dōmo arigatō gozaimashita*. 心より御礼申し上げます。

Daughter Naomi is never backward in telling Dad where his writing leaves a lot to be desired, and my thanks also goes to her for reading through the manuscript and pointing out where corrections were required.

Finally, but certainly not the least, I'd like to thank my wife, Mariko. For more than three decades we have shared a voyage through life that has been both fascinating and enormously fulfilling. Without her unshakable belief in me, I would never have had the courage to break out of my comfort zone and pursue new and at times seemingly insurmountable challenges. Without her by my side, this book would not have happened.

INTRODUCTION

Photograph 1 Beautiful examples of antique *tategu*: Tenryū-ji Temple, Kyoto, Japan

In Japanese construction and architecture, the term *tategu* refers to internal and external doors and windows, and those who make and install *tategu* are called *tateguya*, or *tategushi*.

Besides its purely functional role of closing off or partitioning the internal space, protecting against the elements, providing relief against the harsh sun, and security, *tategu* is the one element of construction that allows a personal decorative touch.

Architectural design of the home — traditional or contemporary, Japanese or Western — allows the owner to make an overall statement, but it's the *tategu* that gives the owner the opportunity to express individual flair, and his or her own personality. Quiet serenity, or a more lively ambience; formal, or family oriented; traditional,

or modern — all moods can be communicated with minor variations in how the *tategu* is designed. And it's the skill of the *tateguya* that can give life to the owner's aspirations.

Above all else, *tategu* has to meet three criteria: it must be light — it should be able to open and close or slide freely without hindrance, and it must not appear heavy, so consideration for design, structure and material relative to its location and function is vital; it must be durable — selection of timber type is crucial so that the *tategu* remains serviceable for many years, but at the same time meets the first criterion; and it must be attractive — beauty in structure, material and form within the first two criteria are essential elements for conveying the desired

1

atmosphere or mood. All three criteria are addressed in this book.

The shoji doors and windows we are familiar with in the West are just one part of the *tateguya*'s craft, albeit a very important part. The vast range of structures and designs that can be incorporated into shoji perhaps more than any other element of *tategu* allows tremendous scope for a distinctive feel and functionality within a room or other living space. The term shoji itself means something that "blocks off" (light) or "obstructs" (a view).

I first came into contact with Japanese culture when studying the language in 1974, and very quickly became captivated by the Japanese sense of aesthetics, shoji in particular. The paper backing in shoji fills the room with a gentle soft light, and introduces an element of ambiguity so valued by the Japanese. The play of light and shadows on the paper allows the outline to be discerned, but not clearly enough to be identified. The object can be seen, but not seen.

Shoji are much more than just thin pieces of wood held in a frame with paper stuck on the back. To the Japanese they are a way of life, a constant that has been a part of their character for almost a thousand years, and even amid the present gradual trend away from traditional Japanese style houses, the sense of warmth and comfort projected by shoji ensures that they will remain within the Japanese spirit for centuries to come.

This is a book about shoji, specifically, how to make basic shoji.

In formulating the structure of the book, I wanted to provide enough options that would enable woodworkers to make a set of shoji through which they could express their own individuality without making the process overly complex. I've tried to keep the instructions clear and to the point, but I've also added snippets of information where I thought they would be helpful or of interest.

This is not a book of photographs of shoji, nor is it about the spiritual aesthetics of shoji. There are many glossy colored photograph books present-

ing a range of beautiful shoji amid ideal settings whose photographs and descriptions are much more elegant than anything I would be able to present.

I do, however, provide a large number of photographs and diagrams explaining exactly how to make the shoji and kumiko patterns I've included, which is the primary aim of this book.

Moreover, I do not attempt to give advice on how to tear down and reinstall a door or window frame to fit the shoji you make. Window and door frames are different from country to country, and from region to region, so if you are not confident that you have the necessary knowledge or experience, you should hire a qualified carpenter to do this framing work for you. The information provided in this book will enable you to give the carpenter clear instructions on the groove measurements.

Without the expensive and high-tech machinery available to the larger *tategu* businesses in Japan, and by the very nature of shoji and kumiko work, woodworkers in the West must rely heavily on hand tools and their hand skills when building shoji, as *shokunin* had to do in the past before the advent of modern technology and computer-controlled accuracy. Shoji and kumiko work requires extremely high levels of accuracy, and precise joinery, so as a prelude to the first shoji I list a series of exercises that I strongly recommend you complete to give you practice in the hand skills necessary for cutting the joints in shoji frames and kumiko.

These exercises will very quickly let you know about your cutting techniques and the areas you need to concentrate on so that the joinery in your shoji and the internal kumiko is straight, square and tight.

I then give detailed instructions on making a set of standard shoji doors (scaled down), covering all processes from calculating dimensions, preparing the frame and cutting the kumiko, through to attaching shoji paper and fitting the shoji into its grooves, including minor adjustments necessary so that it sits flush with the side pillars.

I also discuss some of the variations you can apply to the shoji joinery to make them more distinctive, and I give a comprehensive list of jigs for you to make that will help you work more accurately and efficiently.

After the standard shoji, I give a detailed step-by-step guide on making a shoji with a hip-board, a slightly more complex kumiko pattern, and a variation on the rail/stile joinery.

In the third set of shoji, I lay the groundwork for a very attractive design in the next book — *kōzu* — and introduce the *izutsu-tsunagi*, a relatively simple and straightforward kumiko pattern.

Following this, I explain two other kumiko patterns — the *futae kaku-tsunagi*, and the *asa-no-ha*, including the four different ways of making the *asa-no-ha*. These form the basis for many other more intricate patterns. This is the fun part of shoji, and I give detailed instructions and dimensioned diagrams for each.

However, before we embark on our journey into the fascinating — and at times frustrating — world of shoji, I will devote some pages to the Japanese hand plane — the *kanna*. For the vast majority of my shoji and kumiko work, I use Japanese tools, and apart from the use of a Western block plane in some jigs, I only use Japanese planes.

The *kanna* is an outstanding tool, but it can be very difficult to set up and maintain. Many woodworkers in the West have tried *kanna*, only to give up in understandable exasperation when they could not get it to work properly.

Therefore in the first part of this book I cover all aspects of the *kanna* at length, specifically the four main types I use for the shoji detailed in this book. This will give you a basic understanding of how to set up a new *kanna*, and how to maintain it at its peak performance. Hopefully this should help to dispel many of the myths surrounding *kanna* that have grown out of simple frustration.

Photograph 2 A very simple shoji used to great effect

PART 1 — *KANNA*

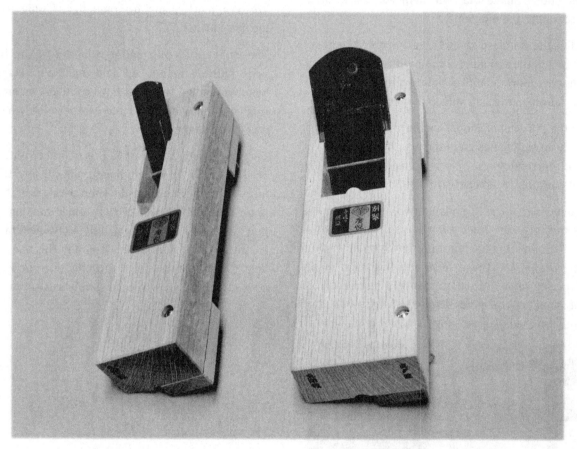

Photograph 3 Set of *inrō kanna* — for shaping the meeting edges of shoji

OVERVIEW

Perhaps more than any other tool, the *kanna* symbolizes the tradition, pride and skill of the Japanese *shokunin*. A well-tuned and well-maintained *kanna* and a properly sharpened blade can take shavings measured in microns, and leave a glistening, mirror-like surface that requires no further work or processing.

The major difference between Japanese and Western planes is that *kanna* are pulled, whereas Western planes are used with a pushing action. For woodworkers used to Western planes, the pulling action of the *kanna* can make it quite difficult to control. The wooden body of the *kanna* does, however, provide greater direct feedback from the workpiece than the metal Western plane does, so any right- or left-hand bias in the planing action can be readily felt, and easily corrected.

The wooden-bodied *kanna* (*dai-kanna*) first appeared in Japan during the mid-fifteenth century from China. Before then, Japanese carpenters used the *yari-ganna*, a plane shaped like a spear (*yari*) and used with a pulling action (it is still very occasionally used for special needs in temple and shrine construction and architecture). The planing process with the *yari-ganna* was controlled entirely by subtle hand movements, so the quality of the finish depended entirely on the skill of the *shokunin*.

The newly introduced *kanna* were referred to as *tsuki-kanna* to differentiate them from the *yari-ganna*. They were fitted with handles and pushed in the same way they were used in China, but before long, they were modified so they could be used with a pulling action, as is the case today.

The main reason for this modification is that Japanese *shokunin* worked in a sitting position, and more force could be applied to the plane with a pulling rather than pushing action. This new plane and the pulling action enabled *shokunin* to take much finer and more consistent shavings, and therefore perform much finer work. It also paved the way for much more detailed kumiko work and designs in shoji.

At first glance, the *kanna* may appear to be a very simple device — a blade and chip-breaker held securely in place within a wooden block (*dai*). A closer look, though, reveals a highly complex integration of angles, grooves and wedges. Blades are laminated with a thin piece of hard steel, which forms the cutting edge, and a thicker backing of softer metal. These blades are hand-forged, so there will always be subtle differences between blades. The *dai* is therefore made to fit the blade, and a quality combination of the two requires great skill by the blacksmith and the *dai* maker.

Once a Western plane has been properly tuned, very little subsequent maintenance is required, other than the regular sharpening of the blade. However, this is not the case for *kanna*. The *dai* is made of wood (normally Japanese red or white oak) and the laminated blade has a hollowed back, so the *kanna* requires constant maintenance and tuning. This requirement for regular conditioning is perhaps the main source of the myth that *kanna* are difficult to use.

Changes in weather and humidity will affect the *dai*, and, naturally, the function of the *kanna*, but tuning to bring it back to its peak performance need only take a couple of minutes.

Conditioning the blade is one area that can be terrifying to woodworkers new to Japanese planes. The *kanna* blade has a very narrow flat at the back of the cutting edge in front of the hollow, and after repeated sharpening, this flat will eventually disappear. Before this flat disappears, the front edge of the hollow must be pushed out to create a new flat by striking the soft metal with a hammer. With the appropriate knowledge and sufficient care, and if you follow the processes detailed in this book, this need not be such a frightening experience.

KANNA ANATOMY

The following diagrams show the various parts of a *kanna* and blade. Throughout the book, I'll tend to use the English term in cases where a reasonable English equivalent exists, and the Japanese term in cases where an English term sounds too convoluted or unnatural.

Kanna terminology can at times be somewhat confusing to say the least. Internal travel controls and regional isolation through history coupled with local *shokunin* pride have led to multiple names for the same part, and even in some cases the same name for different parts, especially between the Kanto region, centering on Tokyo, and the Kansai region, centering on Osaka. In this book, I'll tend to use the Kanto terminology, but I will also give alternative terms where there is a possibility of some confusion.

Dai

The *kanna dai* is made from Japanese white or red oak blocks that have been acclimatized for several years to minimize wood movement or distortion. Blocks have flat- (plain), quarter- or rift-sawn grain orientation, and each has its advantages and disadvantages.

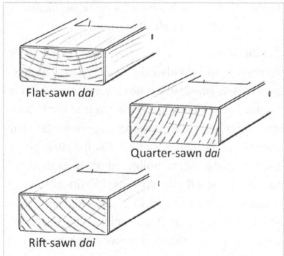

Flat-sawn *dai*

Quarter-sawn *dai*

Rift-sawn *dai*

Diagram 1 Types of *dai*

The flat-sawn *dai* tends to wear away faster than the other two types, but is not as prone to splitting. The quarter-sawn *dai* is resistant to

wear and tends not to warp, but it can split more easily. The rift-sawn *dai* falls between these two.

As with most aspects of woodworking, *shokunin* have their own preferences for the type of *dai* they use, often based on the climate in their region.

Dai for quality *kanna* are made individually for each blade by hand using traditional methods, but when a large number of the same size *dai* is required, for example for schools or less expensive standard *kanna*, the *dai* maker will speed up the process by using a special machine with cutting blades set at the appropriate angles to chisel out the *dai* opening.

The blade bedding angle, or pitch, can vary according to the type or hardness of the wood being planed. Most of the timber used in Japan is softwood (e.g. *kiri* (paulownia), *sugi* (Japanese cedar), *hinoki* (Japanese cypress), and, especially for *tategu*, yellow cedar), so the most common pitch is 31–38°. *Dai* made for use with moderately hard wood (e.g. Japanese oak, *keyaki* (zelkova), and ash) have a pitch of 39–42°, while *dai* for very hard wood (e.g. ebony, teak and rosewood) have a pitch of 45° or greater.

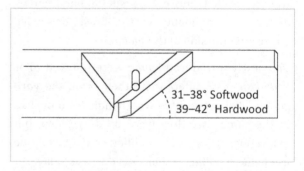

31–38° Softwood
39–42° Hardwood

Diagram 2 Bedding angle (cutaway illustration of the *dai*)

6

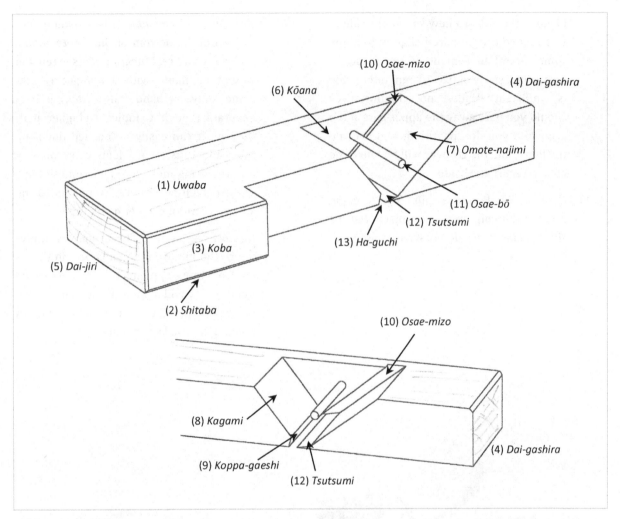

Diagram 3 *Dai* anatomy

(1) *Dai-uwaba* (or simply *uwaba*) — Top of the plane. This is always the heartwood side.

(2) *Dai-shitaba* (or simply *shitaba*) — Sole of the plane. This is always the sapwood side. I discuss the various profiles for the sole in the *hira-ganna* section, and maintenance of the sole in the maintenance section.

(3) *Dai-koba* (or simply *koba*) — Side of the plane.

(4) *Dai-gashira* — Front. On Western planes, this would equate to the back of the plane.

(5) *Dai-jiri* — Back. Similarly, on Western planes, this would equate to the front.

(6) *Kōana* — The v-shaped opening in the *uwaba* from where the plane shavings are removed.

(7) *Omote-najimi* (also called *senaka-najimi*) — This is the part of the *dai* that supports the body of the blade, and normally requires some form of adjustment on new *kanna*.

(8) *Kagami* — The angled face opposite the *omote-najimi*.

(9) *Koppa-gaeshi* — The bottom part of the *kagami* that is angled back and opens up to the mouth. This reverse-angled part allows shavings to enter the *kōana* and exit the plane freely. Over time, constant sole conditioning will eventually make the mouth too wide, and corrective action will be required.

(10) *Osae-mizo* — Side groove. This is a wedge-shaped groove that secures the sides of the

blade to the *dai*. In a new *kanna*, the side of this groove can be pared slightly to allow some lateral movement of the blade — normally a space of 0.5–1.0 mm either side is sufficient. Under no circumstances should you pare away the upper part of the groove. If you do this, the fit will become too loose, and the grooves will no longer be able to secure the blade.

(11) *Osae-bō* — Pressure pin. The *osae-bō* secures the chip-breaker in place. *Dai* for single-blade *kanna* do not have an *osae-bō*.

(12) *Tsutsumi* — The *tsutsumi* is a small extension from the bottom of the *omote-najimi*, and serves no real function. This extension cannot be made with a *dai*-cutting machine, only on hand-crafted *dai*, so it is generally thought to indicate a higher quality tool. It can easily be pushed down by the blade, causing problems when planing and requiring more frequent conditioning. The *tsutsumi* eventually disappears as the sole is conditioned over many times.

(13) *Ha-guchi* — Mouth. The principles applying to the mouth of a *kanna* are no different from those applying to a Western plane mouth — a wider mouth opening is used for rough planing, and a tighter mouth opening for final smoothing.

Photograph 4 *Hikōki kanna* — for planing kumiko to correct thickness

Blade assembly

Most *kanna* used today are double-blade, that is, the blade assembly consists of the blade (*kanna-ba*, *kanna-ho*, or *kanna-mi*), and the chip-breaker (*uragane*). Until the very early 1900s, all *kanna* were single-blade with no chip-breaker, but with the growing Western influence from the late 1800s, the idea of the chip-breaker was adopted from Western planes at the turn of the century. The early chip-breakers were an oak wedge.

Although more difficult to use, the single-blade *kanna* has its advantages — there is less resistance when planing, it leaves a beautiful polished surface finish, it is highly suited to planing top-quality softwood and hardwood, and it works extremely well in end-grain and cross-grain planing. Its main disadvantage is that in the hands of anyone but the most skilled *shokunin*, tear-out is very difficult to control. They are still available and are still widely used.

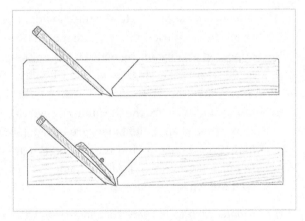

Diagram 4 Single- and double-blade *kanna*

These days, however, double-blade *kanna* are more popular and more common. Resistance while planing is greater than with the single-blade *kanna*, and the quality of the planed surface certainly drops, but these disadvantages are more than offset by the function of the chip-breaker — as in Western planes, the chip-breaker helps to prevent tear-out and produce an acceptable surface finish in difficult wood, so this type of *kanna* can also be used effectively by less-skilled *shokunin*.

Kanna blades are a lamination of a thin layer of hard high-carbon steel or in some cases high-speed steel (*hagane*) and a thicker backing of softer iron (*jigane*). The blade forms a wedge in thickness and also in width from top (*atama*) to the bottom (*uraba*), so that as the blade is dropped into the *dai* it locks in securely, and from there it is tapped down to the required projection. Chip-breakers usually have the same lamination structure as blades, although some are made from solid steel.

There are also *kanna* that use short replaceable blades fitted to a special holder. The blades are thrown away rather than sharpened when they become dull. These would be acceptable for general planing, but not for finish planing, where the quality of the finished surface is paramount.

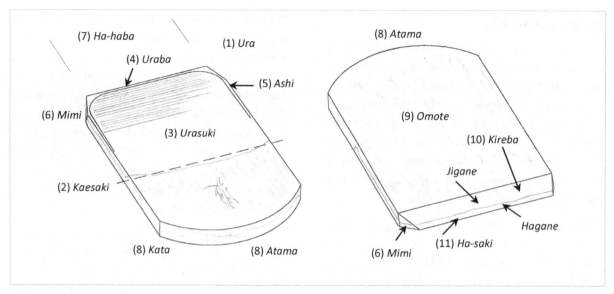

Diagram 5 Blade anatomy

(1) *Ura* — This is the "back" of the blade. Blacksmiths place their mark in the upper section in the softer metal.

(2) *Kaesaki* — This is the boundary between the hard steel (*hagane*) and soft metal (*jigane*) lamination.

(3) *Urasuki* — The hollow. This is perhaps the main characteristic of Japanese plane blades (and chisels). The main function of the *urasuki* is to make it easier to keep the *ura* flat near the cutting edge.

(4) *Uraba* — This is the flat area forming one side of the cutting edge. One look at the shape of *uraba* will give a clear indication of how well or how poorly the blade has been maintained. On a properly maintained blade the *uraba* should be very narrow; a broad *uraba* indicates poor technique. I cover this in much more detail in the *Ito-ura* section from Page 42.

(5) *Ashi* — These are the flat sides of the *urasuki* extending around from the *uraba*. Similar to the *uraba*, the shape of the two *ashi* clearly indicates good or poor technique. This will be covered extensively with the *uraba* in a later section.

(6) *Mimi* — Ears. The ends of the cutting edge are removed to reduce the blade width to its optimum cutting width relative to the mouth of the *dai*. These angled edges are called *mimi*.

(7) *Ha-haba* — Blade width at the cutting edge.

(8) *Atama* and *kata* — Head and shoulders. Over the centuries different shapes have appeared as a means by which blacksmiths could express a degree of individuality. These days the three main shapes for the *atama* and *kata* are the Yoshihiro design (a semi-circle shape), the Chiyozuru design (a higher, oval shape), and the Ishidō design (a much flatter shape). All are named after well-known blacksmiths of the past.

(9) *Omote* (also called *senaka*, and *kō*) — This is the "front" of the blade. This part contacts and is supported by the *dai* at the *omote-najimi*. After forging the blade, the blacksmith shaves the surface of the *omote* with a shaving tool known as a *sen* to give it a slightly concave profile.

(10) *Kireba* — Bevel. As a general rule, the bevel angle is 25°–28° for softwood, and 29°–30° for harder timbers.

(11) *Ha-saki* — Cutting edge.

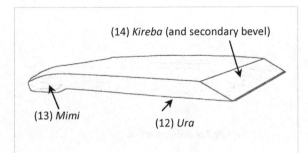

Diagram 6 Chip-breaker (*uragane*)

(12) *Ura* — This is the side of the chip-breaker that contacts the blade *ura*.

(13) *Mimi* — On the chip-breaker, the *mimi* are the parts that are bent so the chip-breaker applies tension to the blade.

(14) *Kireba* — Bevel. Similar to the blade bevel, the chip-breaker bevel is also ground and honed to an angle of 25°–30°. The chip-breaker bevel, however, is also given a slight secondary bevel of around 40°–50°, but this can vary according to personal preferences or the type of timber being planed.

The edge of the chip-breaker is set at about 0.1–0.2 mm from the cutting edge of the blade for finish planing, but for rough planing where surface finish is not as critical, it can be set back up to 0.9 mm from the blade cutting edge.

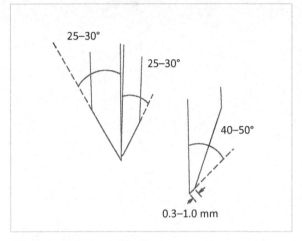

Diagram 7 Bevel angles

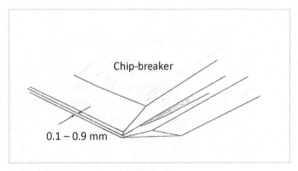

Diagram 8 Blade and chip-breaker setting

11

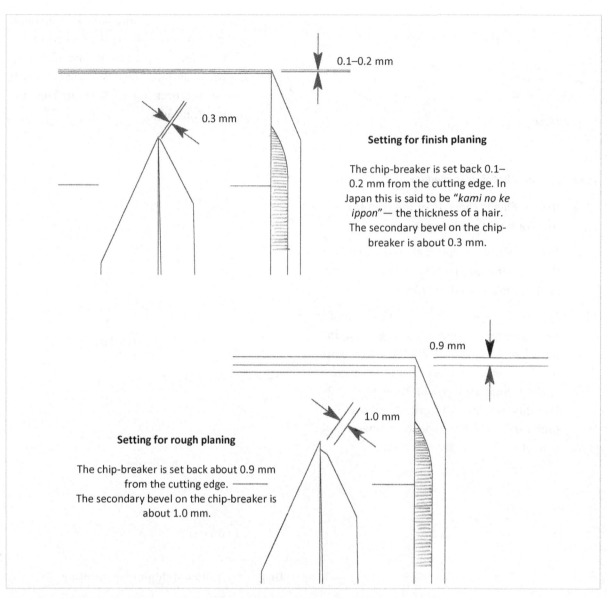

0.1–0.2 mm

0.3 mm

Setting for finish planing

The chip-breaker is set back 0.1–0.2 mm from the cutting edge. In Japan this is said to be *"kami no ke ippon"* — the thickness of a hair. The secondary bevel on the chip-breaker is about 0.3 mm.

0.9 mm

1.0 mm

Setting for rough planing

The chip-breaker is set back about 0.9 mm from the cutting edge. ——— The secondary bevel on the chip-breaker is about 1.0 mm.

Diagram 9 Blade and chip-breaker settings for finish and rough planing

TYPES OF *KANNA*

As with Western planes, Japanese *kanna* come in a multitude of varieties, ranging from the most widely used *hira-ganna*, to highly specialized planes that have a single purpose. In shoji and kumiko work, the *ha-ganna* range of planes fall into this latter category.

In this section, I'll look at the four main types of *kanna* that you are likely to use in the shoji work covered in this book. While I have a bias toward *kanna*, I must emphasize that you do not need to use *kanna* in making the shoji I describe. You will be able to make all of the shoji in this book with Western planes. Western planes do not, however, give the same highly polished surface you can achieve using *kanna*, so if you intend to leave your shoji with a hand-planed finish, as is traditionally done in Japan, *kanna* will give you superior results. If you intend to use sandpaper or apply coats of finish to your shoji, Western planes are quite adequate.

Photograph 5 Some of the joinery possible with specialist kumiko *kanna* (*ha-ganna*)

13

Hira-ganna

Photograph 6 70 mm *hira-ganna*

Hira-ganna (smoothing planes) are the work-horse of Japanese woodworking, and come in a range of sizes for various purposes. The most common size used in Japan is perhaps the 70 mm *kanna*. Metric *kanna* sizes represent the blade width. The largest standard *hira-ganna* is 80 mm, and the sizes range down to the smallest at 36 mm. Much larger *kanna* can be specially ordered, and much smaller *kanna* are also available, but their functions are more specialized and not required in normal shoji work.

If you are thinking of buying your first *kanna*, I would suggest a slightly smaller size of about 55 mm. The 70 mm *kanna* can be somewhat difficult to set up and maintain properly and control when planing until you become accustomed to the different feel, and the 55 mm *kanna* will help you ease into the larger version at a later stage.

Blade width (mm)	Cutting edge (mm)	*Dai* length (approx.) (mm)
80	70	303
70	63	290
65	57	290
60	54	270
55	48	242
50	44	212
48	43	166–172
42	36	166–172
36	31	166–172

Table 1 *Kanna* **sizes**

Blade set-up

Similar to blades in Western planes, blades in the *hira-ganna* are cambered to a greater or lesser degree depending on the type of planing you intend to do. Blades in *kanna* for rough planing (*ara-shikō*) are quite heavily cambered and the *dai* has a wide mouth opening to allow the thick shavings to exit freely. It leaves a fairly coarse finish. The edge of the chip-breaker can be set up to about 0.9 mm from the cutting edge of the blade.

The camber is slightly less on *kanna* used for intermediate planing (*chū-shikō*) and the mouth opening is tighter. The surface is left smooth with only very shallow waves. I set the edge of the chip-breaker on my *chū-shikō kanna* at about 0.2 mm from the blade cutting edge.

For finish planing (*jō-shikō*) the blade of the *jō-shikō kanna* (also called *shiage-kanna*) has minimal camber, and the mouth opening is very tight. The chip-breaker is set 0.1–0.2 mm from the blade cutting edge. If the *chū-shikō kanna* has been set and used properly, only one or two strokes of the *shiage-kanna* is necessary. This plane is tuned to the highest level and special care is given when sharpening the blade so that the planed surface is very smooth and highly polished. This is the plane that highlights a *shokunin's* skill.

Sole set-up

The sole (*shitaba*) on a *hira-ganna* is not flat, rather, areas are recessed so there are two or three contact surfaces depending on the type of planing, and also on the type of work being done. The recessed areas between the contact surfaces are deeper for rough planing, and much shallower for finish planing.

Shokunin tend to have their own preferences for sole conditioning, but as a general rule, it's probably best to have three contact surfaces on *chū-shikō kanna* and *shiage-kanna* when planing narrow material, such as rails and stiles, so the *kanna* remains stable for longer with greater control, and there is less tendency to dip at the end after the *dai-jiri* contact surface passes the edge of the material. This accuracy is especially important considering the joinery at the end or near the end of the rails and stiles. The majority of planing in shoji is this kind of work.

On wider board stock, though, this is somewhat less of a concern and the gliding action of the *kanna* as it moves past the end of the material is more than adequate. Furniture makers tend to plane more board or wider material for tops, panels and the like, so their *kanna* generally have two contact surfaces.

Diagram 10 on the next page shows the two main sole profiles and their uses.

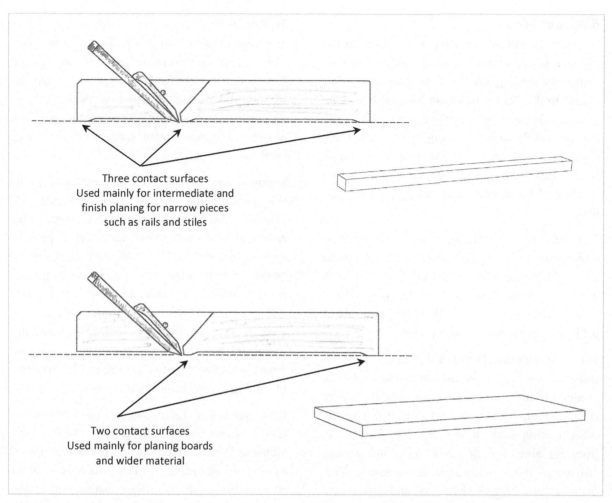

Three contact surfaces
Used mainly for intermediate and
finish planing for narrow pieces
such as rails and stiles

Two contact surfaces
Used mainly for planing boards
and wider material

Diagram 10 Sole profiles

As with all aspects of woodworking, there are many ways to achieve the same end, and planing with a *kanna* is no different. The above diagrams are meant as a guide only. Some *shokunin* prefer three contact surfaces for all planing, others prefer only two. Some will have a flat recessed area on the *dai-gashira*, others will have the edge of the *dai-gashira* curving up slightly. The way that works for you is the best way.

The extent of the recessed area depends on the type of planing being done — more for coarser work, less for finer work.

Dainaoshi kanna

Photograph 7 *Dainaoshi kanna*

The *dainaoshi kanna* is used to condition or tune the sole. The plane itself is a very simple design, and very easy to use, provided the blade has been properly sharpened and set in the *dai*. It consists of a blade, with no chip-breaker, set in a *dai* at 90°, or in some cases 100°. The sole of the *dai* is flat. It is used by scraping across the grain in the areas of the sole that need to be recessed.

Downward pressure while scraping should only be quite light, and the scrapings that may become lodged between the blade and *koppa-gaeshi* should be cleaned out regularly. The blade is set at an angle rather than perpendicular to the

Photograph 8 Scraping the sole of a *kanna*

sides so there is a slight slicing action in the scraping process. The blade should be sharpened straight across, and it should be sharpened frequently because the scraping action dulls it very quickly.

In the past *shokunin* would convert old *hira-ganna* that had worn down into *dainaoshi kanna* by reducing the width of the blade and reseating it in the *dai*.

In English-language articles this *kanna* is often translated as a scraping plane, but it's not suited for use as the kind of scraping plane or cabinet scraper we in the West are used to using.

The only purpose and function of this *kanna* is to condition the sole, and it does this extremely well.

The bottom edges of the *dainaoshi kanna* are often adjusted to suit the user's work methods. A new *dainaoshi kanna* has generally the same sole/side chamfer as a normal *hira-ganna*, but this is not the optimum profile, as it's hard to see clearly where the blade is scraping, and this could cause unwanted scraping in the contact surfaces, or worse still, damage to the *kanna* blade.

Two effective ways of gaining a clearer view of the blade action on the sole of the *kanna* being conditioned are to increase the chamfer to just past the edges of the mouth opening, or to cut a rebate up to just past the edges of the mouth, and just short of the blade's cutting edge.

I use the former on my *dainaoshi kanna* because it's the simplest way, but the latter is also a very good method. The following diagram shows these profiles.

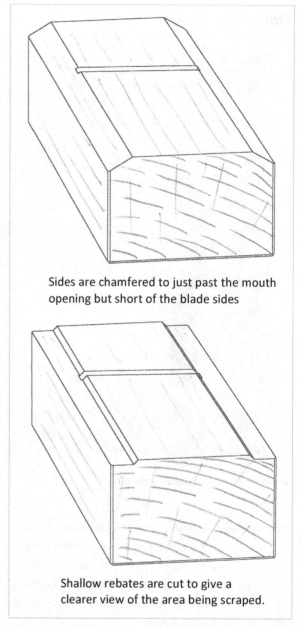

Sides are chamfered to just past the mouth opening but short of the blade sides

Shallow rebates are cut to give a clearer view of the area being scraped.

Diagram 11 Sole profiles for *dainaoshi kanna*

Kiwa-ganna

Photograph 9 Left and right pair of *kiwa-ganna*

The *kiwa-ganna* are rebate (rabbet) planes, or shoulder planes. They are used to cut rebates, and come in left- and right-side cutting styles, so planing can always be with the grain.

The blade is angled in the *dai* so that the edge of the blade which forms an acute angle is in line with the side of the *dai*. This enables the *kanna* to plane corners and edges with high precision, while the angled blade also provides a clean cross-grain cut.

While the *kiwa-ganna* may look a fairly simple plane, it is in fact very difficult to set up and tune.

Photograph 10 *Kiwa-ganna*

New *kiwa-ganna* are seldom, if ever, usable without extensive conditioning, and the skill required in tuning and adjusting this plane is much greater than that required for a *hira-ganna*. When projected to the correct cutting depth, the cutting edge must be exactly parallel to the sole, and the blade corner must be in line with the side of the *dai*.

For each plane and blade, there is only one correct angle where the cutting edge meets the side of the blade for these two requirements to be met, and this angle must be exact — it cannot be too acute or too obtuse otherwise the plane does not perform at its optimum.

Great care is therefore essential in the initial blade adjustment process to achieve this angle, and in all subsequent sharpening processes to ensure it is maintained. In addition, shavings can tend to become jammed between the blade corner and the side of the *dai*, so

19

modifications often need to be made in this area as well.

Unfortunately, because of the difficulty and time required in setting up these planes, all too often they are thrown into the corner of a box and rarely pulled out for use.

The following steps will help you to tune your *kiwa-ganna* and hopefully avoid the frustration of trying to use a plane that refuses to work. These steps apply to both right-side and left-side planes.

Initial tuning

(1)   Flatten the sole using sandpaper (about 220-240 grit) attached to a flat piece of MDF or hard timber.

(2)   Ensure that the inner side of the plane with the blade opening (blade side) is exactly perpendicular to the sole. If it is not at 90°, use a sharp plane to shave off just enough from the side to square it. This step must be done before any adjustment is done to the blade, because if you alter the side after you adjust the blade, the geometry has been changed and you will need to adjust the blade again.

(3)   Insert the blade (without the chip-breaker) and tap it down until the cutting edge at the acute angle corner projects the correct amount for normal planing.

(4)   Laterally adjust the blade so that the acute angle corner is in line with the side of the plane (a very slight amount of projection past the side is acceptable), while adjusting the depth of the blade so that the acute angle corner remains at the correct planing depth.

(5)   Sight along the sole of the plane from the *dai-jiri* to check whether the cutting edge is parallel to the sole. If the cutting edge is parallel, congratulations, you've virtually won the lottery. You can jump straight to the adjustment of the chip-breaker. More than likely it's not parallel, so you'll need to continue.

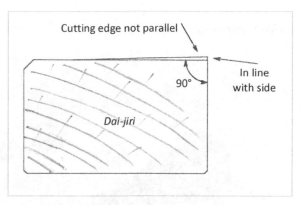

Diagram 12 Tuning *kiwa-ganna* 01

(6)   If it's not parallel, check which side of the cutting edge projects more. You have to remove metal from the side that projects more; i.e. the acute angle side or the obtuse angle side.

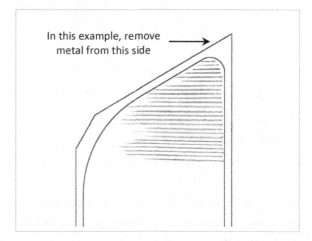

Diagram 13 Tuning *kiwa-ganna* 02

(7)   Using a coarse sharpening stone (I use a 220 grit stone), carefully remove metal from the side that projected more from the sole. You should adhere to all the proper sharpening techniques, and simply apply greater pressure on the appropriate side. This should be a gradual and steady process, and reinsert the blade into the *dai* regularly to check for parallel.

(8)   As the cutting edge becomes closer to parallel, change to a less coarse stone (about a 1,000 grit stone) so you don't remove too much. If you find that you need to remove a large amount of metal, you may also have to tap out the blade to prevent *uragire*. For this, simply follow the normal

20

tapping out procedures I describe in the tapping out section (see Pages 38–41). This can be a laborious process, but the more careful you are here, the better the plane will perform.

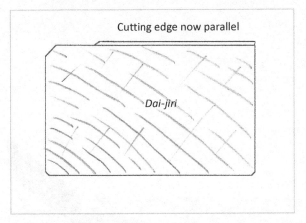

Diagram 14 Tuning *kiwa-ganna* **03**

(9) Once the cutting edge is parallel to the sole, make any necessary adjustment to the *mi-mi* on the grinder, then sharpen the blade as normal. Be careful not to alter the cutting edge angle.

(10) Insert the blade and tap down to the normal cutting depth, making sure that acute angle corner is in line with the side of the plane. Recheck that the cutting edge is parallel to the sole. If it's not, go back to step 6. If it is parallel, continue on.

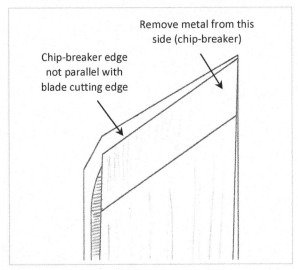

Diagram 15 Tuning *kiwa-ganna* **04**

(11) Insert the chip-breaker and tap down until the edge reaches about 1 mm from the blade cutting edge. Check that the chip-breaker edge is parallel to the cutting edge. If it's not parallel, use the coarse stone and remove the necessary amount of metal from the appropriate side. Again, you should adhere to the normal sharpening techniques, and work carefully so you don't remove too much. This part can be quite awkward, because the blade is housed in the *osae-mizo*, but the chip-breaker isn't, so the blade and chip-breaker sides aren't parallel.

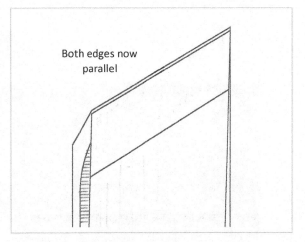

Diagram 16 Tuning *kiwa-ganna* **05**

(12) When the edge becomes parallel, hone the chip-breaker bevel as normal.

(13) Check that the chip-breaker sits tightly against the blade and adjust as necessary, following the procedure I describe in the section on adjusting the chip-breaker (from Page 29).

(14) Reinsert the blade and chip-breaker into the *dai*, and condition the sole as required. The profile of the sole is a personal preference, but the concave areas between the contact surfaces should only be very shallow.

Despite their temperamental character and the difficulty in adjusting and maintaining them to their peak performance, properly tuned *kiwa-ganna* are wonderful planes to use, and they do their job extremely well.

These planes, or their Western equivalent, will be needed to make minor adjustments to the depth and width of the rebates in the top and bottom rails in the shoji we make later in the book.

Side opening may need to be expanded to allow shavings to pass more freely

Side opening

Photograph 11 Tuning *kiwa-ganna* 06

Kakumen-ganna

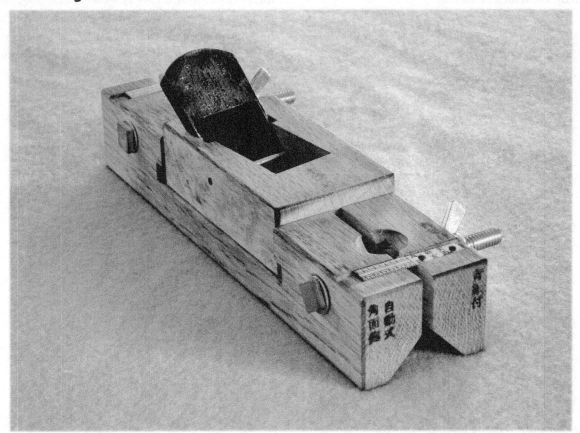

Photograph 12 *Kakumen-ganna*

The *kakumen-ganna* consists of a very small *kanna* secured in two parallel fences attached to each other with bolts, nuts and wing nuts and each set at 45° on the underside to form a 90° angle. Adjusting the wing nuts allows one of the fences to move in and out freely so the size of the chamfer can be increased or decreased.

The *dai* is held in these two fences in grooves, and can be moved along these grooves so the entire blade can be used. The blade itself is set in the *dai* at an angle so it cuts in a slicing action, resulting in a glistening chamfer surface. These days a brass plate is attached to the sole of the *dai* to protect the sole surface. When the blade needs to be sharpened, the *dai* is simply removed from the fences, and the blade removed and sharpened as in a normal *hira-ganna*.

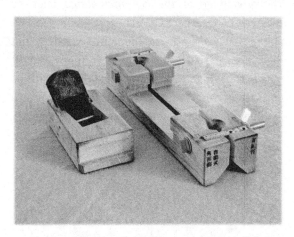

Photograph 13 *Kakumen-ganna* fence and *dai*

Another name that is frequently used for this plane is *men-tori kanna*, but this normally refers to the chamfer planes with non-adjustable fences and a broader range of edge profiles. The *men-tori kanna* are the Japanese version of the molding planes used in the past before the introduction of the router, and still used by woodworkers who enjoy a quieter workshop.

Highly accurate chamfers will be essential for the kind of rail and stile joinery we use in the shoji we make in this book, so I would encourage you to purchase this plane to make cutting these chamfers and the assembly process much easier and more efficient.

Photograph 16 Markings ensure accuracy and repeatability

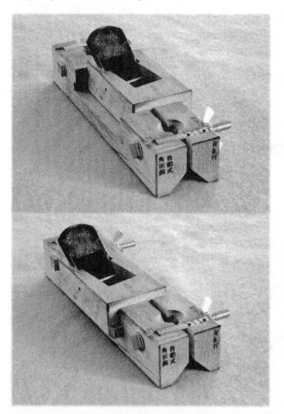

Photograph 14 Entire blade can be used

The advantage of the *kakumen-ganna* over its Western counterparts is that very minor adjustments can be made to the fence settings and therefore the size of the chamfer with just a slight turn of the wing nuts. Moreover, with graduations marked on the front and back of the plane, these settings can be easily and accurately repeated.

Photograph 15 Brass plate on sole

ADJUSTING A NEW PLANE

Although some new *kanna* are sold as "ready to use", in almost all cases, new *kanna* need some form of adjustment before they can be used effectively. Quality *kanna* are created through the collective efforts of highly skilled *shokunin* usually working in completely separate locations, so each *kanna* is different with its own unique "personality".

As a craftsman, I believe this initial adjustment of the *kanna* is a crucial process that gives me the opportunity to get to know the *kanna's* characteristics and mold them to suit my methods of work, and it strengthens my sense of "ownership" of this vital tool. I also know that any mistakes I make here can have an adverse impact on how the *kanna* performs in the long term. In this section I'll simplify this process by breaking it down into its basic steps.

You need the following tools for this:

(1) Sharpening stones (coarse, medium and fine)

(2) Flattening plate (to keep the stones flat)

(3) Hammer (preferably a Japanese *gennō*), or mallet for setting and retracting the blade

(4) 2B pencil

(5) Small and fine metal file with a flat, square end

(6) Chisels (3, 6, 13 mm and wider if required)

(7) Straightedge

(8) *Dainaoshi kanna* (or cabinet scraper)

(9) Sandpaper (220–240 grit) attached to MDF (approx. 600 x 120 mm)

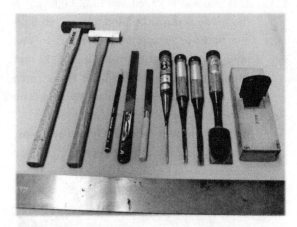

Photograph 17 Some of the tools required for adjusting a new *kanna*

These are the broad steps for the adjustment process and the order in which I carry them out.

• **Flatten the back** — *Ura-oshi* (tap out if required and flatten the back)

• **Adjust the *dai*** (*omote-najimi* and *osae-mizo*) for a secure fitting blade

• **Adjust the chip-breaker** (flatten the back and adjust for a tight fit with the blade)

• **Condition the sole**

• **Test cut** (including any final adjustment)

Before you begin, make sure that your sharpening stones are and remain completely flat throughout this procedure.

Flatten the back

(1) This process is called *ura-oshi*. Lightly rub the blade *ura* on the medium grit stone a few times to determine how flat it is. You only need to flatten the end 10-15 mm from the cutting edge. Check the scratch pattern to see where contact between the stone and the blade has been made. Depending on where contact has been made, you may or may not need to tap out (see the section on tapping out from Page 38 for details of this process).

Photograph 18 Flatten back 01

(2) If even contact has been made almost all the way across the *ura*, you don't need to tap out. If contact is centered on one side and the other side is slightly raised, or contact is on both sides but not in the center, you will need to tap out. Only light tapping should be required — just enough to lower the slightly elevated points.

(3) Rub the *ura* on the medium stone again to check that more even contact is being made with the stone. If so, continue to the next step, otherwise tap out again in the appropriate place.

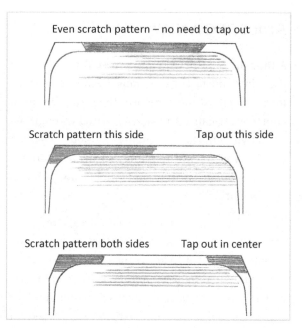

Diagram 17 Flatten back 02

(4) Still on the medium stone, rub the *ura* until even contact is made fully across the blade. Check the *ura* often and stop as soon as full contact has been made. This should not take much more than a few minutes. Any longer and you should tap out again at the elevated points.

(5) Polish the *ura* on the fine stone, ensuring that the polished surface extends the entire width. The *ura* of the blade is now properly flattened, and we can move on to adjusting the *dai* so that the blade fits securely. Don't worry about sharpening the bevel at this stage.

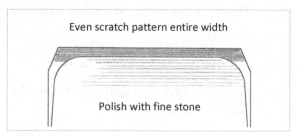

Diagram 18 Flatten back 03

What happens if we don't tap out?

A gap in the scratch pattern indicates that section is slightly elevated. If, say, the scratch pattern is on the left side only, this means the right side is slightly elevated, as can be seen in the diagram on the right.

So to get an even scratch pattern across the blade, we would need to remove the amount of metal shown by the dashed line. Not only is this extra work and effort, but it leaves us with the *ura* shape shown in the bottom diagram.

I discuss other problems with the *ura* from Page 43.

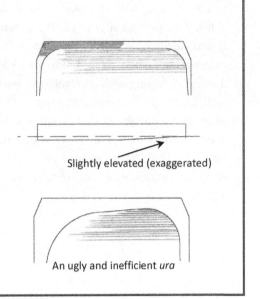

Slightly elevated (exaggerated)

An ugly and inefficient *ura*

Adjust the *dai*

(1) Rub the 2B pencil on the bottom half of the blade *omote* and on both sides so you have an even coverage of graphite.

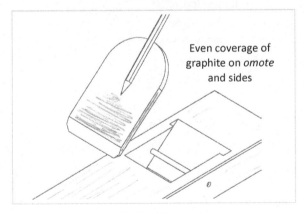

Even coverage of graphite on *omote* and sides

Diagram 19 Adjust *dai* 01

(2) Insert the blade into the *dai*, and lightly tap down with the *gennō* (or mallet). Tap down until the blade meets resistance, then tap the *dai-gashira* to remove the blade. When tapping to remove, or unseat, the blade, tap each side of the *dai-gashira* on the top

chamfered edge. Avoid hitting in the middle part as this could split the *dai*. The tapping should just be firm enough so that the blade is unseated after a few taps, and the angle of tapping should be parallel to the bedding angle of the blade.

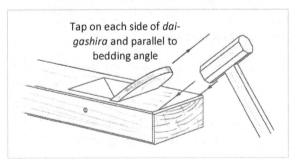

Tap on each side of *dai-gashira* and parallel to bedding angle

Diagram 20 Adjust *dai* 02

(3)   Graphite will be left on the *omote-najimi* and the sides of the *osae-mizo* where contact was made with the blade *omote* and sides. With the end edge of the file, carefully and slowly scrape away the areas on the *omote-najimi* where the graphite marks are darkest. Scraping with a chisel also works well. Do not try to scrape away too much at once, just enough so that a smudge remains in these darker areas. Your eventual aim here is to have an even coverage of graphite marks over the entire *omote-najimi*.

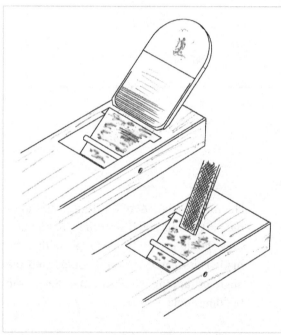

Diagram 21 Adjust *dai* 03

(4)   While scraping the *omote-najimi*, also carefully and lightly remove graphite marks on the sides on the *osae-mizo* with the 3 mm chisel. Do not, however, touch the upper surface of the grooves.

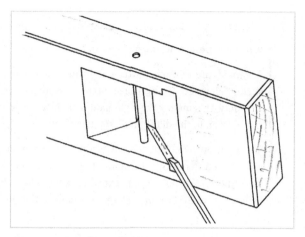

Diagram 22 Adjust *dai* 04

(5)   Rub the pencil over the blade and sides again if necessary, and reinsert the blade into the *dai*. Tap down until the blade meets resistance, then remove. Repeat steps (2) and (3) until you have an even and consistent coverage of graphite on the *omote-najimi*, indicating that the blade is seated firmly in the *dai*.

(6)   Continue lightly scraping the *omote-najimi* until the cutting edge of the blade reaches about 4-5 mm back from the mouth when you push the blade into the *dai* with just hand pressure. Once you've reached this point, stop otherwise the blade will become too loose.

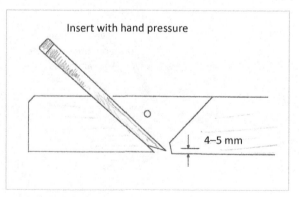

Diagram 23 Adjust *dai* 05

(7) If necessary, continue paring away a small amount from the sides of the *osae-mizo* toward the top of the *kanna* so there is a gap of about 1.0 mm between the sides of the blade and the sides of the *osae-mizo* to allow lateral adjustment of the blade.

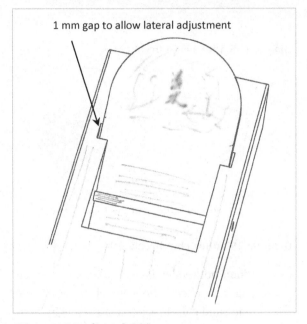

1 mm gap to allow lateral adjustment

Diagram 24 Adjust *dai* 06

(8) Insert the blade with hand pressure, rub the 2B pencil on both sides of the chip-breaker, then insert the chip-breaker as normal on top of the blade and give it a couple of taps with the *gennō*.

(9) Remove both the blade and the chip-breaker, and check the inner sides of the *dai* above the *osae-mizo* for graphite marks left by the chip-breaker.

(10) The lateral fitting of the chip-breaker in the *dai* should not be tight, so using the 6 mm and 13 mm chisels, carefully and lightly pare away the graphite marks.

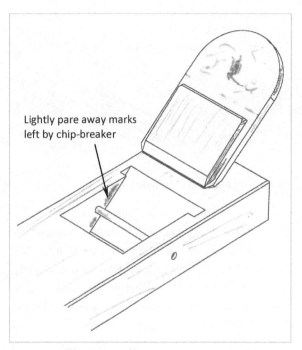

Lightly pare away marks left by chip-breaker

Diagram 25 Adjust *dai* 07

Adjust the chip-breaker

(1) Flatten the chip-breaker *ura* in the same way that you flattened the blade *ura*, including tapping out if necessary. If the *ura* is out to the extent that you need to tap out, work carefully, and give it only a few light taps with the *gennō*.

(2) Sharpen the main bevel at an angle of 25°–30°, then sharpen a secondary bevel at 40°–50°. This secondary bevel angle is only approximate, and can be increased if you prefer.

(3) Lay the blade on a flat solid surface *ura* side up, and place the chip-breaker on the blade *ura* with the cutting edge of the chip-breaker about 1.0 mm back from the blade cutting edge. A properly adjusted and tuned chip-breaker contacts the blade in three areas — the two corners at the back, and the *uraba* at the front.

29

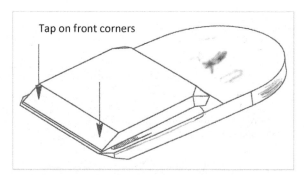

Diagram 26 Adjust chip-breaker 01

(4) Tap the two front corners of the chip-breaker with your fingernail or similar object and listen to the sound. If one side gives a rattling sound, that side is slightly elevated, meaning that the blade and chip-breaker surfaces are not in full and tight contact across the entire width.

(5) In this example (Diagram 27 below), corners A2 are rattling, so there's poor contact (a gap) between the blade *uraba* and chip-breaker at corner A.

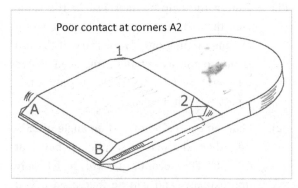

Diagram 27 Adjust chip-breaker 02

(6) Lightly file away a very small amount from the chip-breaker *mimi* on the side of the rattle (in this example, corner 1), and check again. It is very easy to file off too much, so be careful and use a very light touch. If finer tuning is necessary, you can use the medium sharpening stone instead of the file.

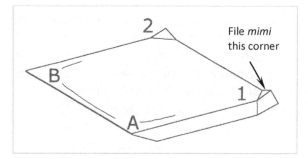

Diagram 28 Adjust chip-breaker 03

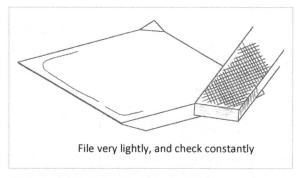

File very lightly, and check constantly

Diagram 29 Adjust chip-breaker 04

(7) When both sides give a solid sound when you tap, check the contact between the blade and chip-breaker against a light. If no light is visible between the two across the entire width, the chip-breaker is properly tuned.

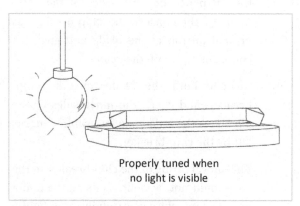

Properly tuned when
no light is visible

Diagram 30 Adjust chip-breaker 05

Condition the sole

(1) Decide on the type of profile you want for your *kanna*. I explained the different sole profiles and uses in the *hira-ganna* section on Pages 15 and 16 (see Diagram 10).

(2) Insert the blade and chip-breaker into the *dai*, and tap down until the blade cutting edge is 1–2 mm back from the mouth. It is important that the blade and chip-breaker are properly set in the *dai*, so that all the normal tension and pressure placed on the *dai* during use are present when the sole is being conditioned.

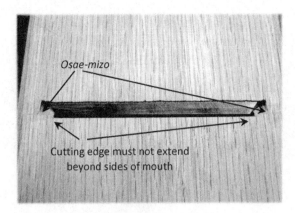

Photograph 19 Condition sole 02

(4) Check the contact between the chip-breaker and the *osae-bō*. If the *osae-bō* has left a noticeable mark on the chip-breaker at any point, lightly file the underside of the *osae-bō* in the area where the contact has been too strong. Do not file away too much; if required this should only need a very light filing.

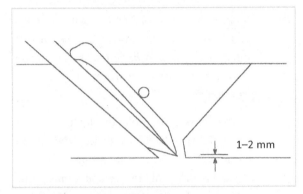

Diagram 31 Condition sole 01

(3) At this point, check that the cutting width of the blade does not extend beyond the sides of the mouth into the end of the *osae-mizo*. If it does, use a grinder or coarse stone to increase the *mimi* on both sides of the blade, thereby reducing the cutting width as required. If it extends beyond the mouth on one side only, increase the *mimi* to reduce the cutting width on that side only.

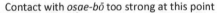

Contact with *osae-bō* too strong at this point

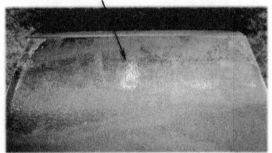

Photograph 20 Condition sole 03

(5) Flatten the sole using sandpaper (about 220–240 grit) attached to a flat, thick board of MDF or hard timber roughly 600 x 120 mm. The sandpaper should cover the width of the board, and at least the front 400 mm (there is no need to cover the entire 600 mm length). Secure the board to a flat workbench. Double-check that the blade and chip-breaker are drawn back at least 1–2 mm from the mouth so they are not marked by the sandpaper. With a normal planing motion and with normal pressure on the sandpaper, move the *kanna* backward and forward along the length of the sandpaper four or five times. Check the

sole, and once there is a full and even coverage of sandpaper marks on the sole, clean off the dust and move on to the next step.

(6)   Check for flatness of the sole with your straightedge against a light in the order shown in Diagram 32 below. If the sole is not perfectly flat, repeat the previous step until it is.

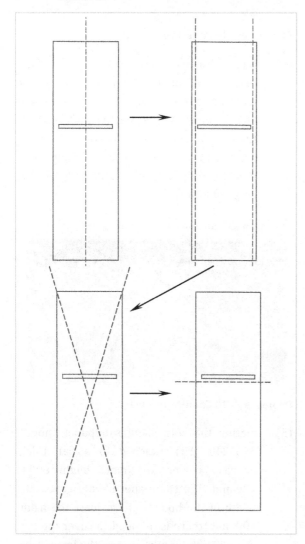

Diagram 32 Condition sole 04

(7)   Pare away a small amount of wood to create a slight recess on both sides of the mouth opening (the areas shown in the following photograph) using the 13 mm (or larger) chisel. This step tends to be easily overlooked, but these small side pieces can raise the cutting edge off the surface and

badly affect the performance of the *kanna*, so avoid any shortcuts here.

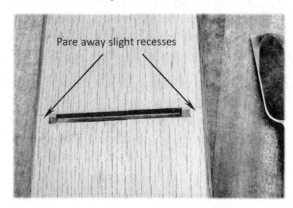

Pare away slight recesses

Photograph 21 Condition sole 05

(8)   Using your *dainaoshi kanna* with a sharp blade (or a normal cabinet scraper if you don't have a *dainaoshi kanna*) scrape away the recessed areas according to your sole preference.

(9)   Scrape across the sole in the area from about 10 mm back from the *dai-jiri* to about 6-8 mm from the mouth opening. For a finishing plane (*shiage-kanna*) this recess needs only to be very slight (no more than about 0.5 mm should be sufficient), whereas for coarser planing, this recess should be slightly deeper. How you intend to use the *kanna* will dictate this.

(10)   Scrape across the sole from about 10 mm back from the *dai-gashira* to the mouth opening if there are three contact surfaces, or from the back of the *dai-gashira* if there are only two contact surfaces.

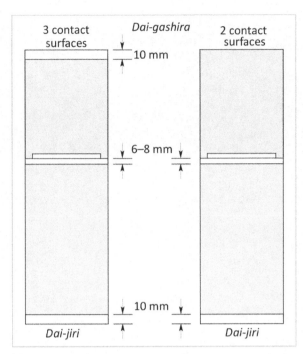

Diagram 33 Condition sole 06

(11) Be very careful when scraping close to the mouth so you don't scratch the *kanna* blade, and you don't extend past the mouth and remove material in the contact surface on the other side. Using a wide chisel to scrape across in the mouth region will give you more control and reduce the risk of this.

Photograph 22 Condition sole 07

(12) Check the sole regularly with the straight-edge as you scrape, and when you're satis-fied that it's contacting the sole only at the three (or two) contact surfaces, give the contact surface next to the mouth a final check with the straightedge to make sure it has remained flat.

Photograph 23 Condition sole 08

Test cut

(1) Remove the blade and sharpen the bevel.

(2) Replace the blade and chip-breaker. Sighting down the sole from the *dai-jiri*, ex-tend the blade enough for a fine shaving, and tap down the chip-breaker so the front edge is about 0.2 mm back from the blade cutting edge. If all the previous steps have been followed correctly, you should be able to take off the thinnest of shavings from the test piece.

(3) If you can't take a thin shaving, the most likely problem is the *tsutsumi*. As you ex-tended the blade cutting edge past the mouth to plane the test piece, the in-creased tension on the *tsutsumi* may have pushed it down slightly, thereby raising the cutting edge off the test piece surface.

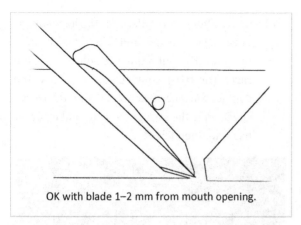

OK with blade 1–2 mm from mouth opening.

Diagram 34 Test cut 01

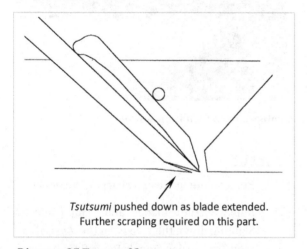

Tsutsumi pushed down as blade extended.
Further scraping required on this part.

Diagram 35 Test cut 02

(4)   In this case, retract the blade slightly, and carefully scrape away more from *dai-gashira* side of the mouth with a chisel. As I mentioned earlier, the *tsutsumi* serves no real purpose, so you can scrape away a reasonable amount, but be very careful not to scratch the blade.

(5)   You should now be able to take very fine shavings.

SHARPENING

It goes without saying that no matter how well you have tuned your *kanna* and regardless of the quality of the blade, if the blade is not sharp it will not cut properly.

Sharpening by experienced Japanese *shokunin* is a display of concentration and efficiency. Their actions and movements are quick but unhurried, and they constantly examine the blade to determine how well the stone is cutting and whether any corrective pressure on different parts of the blade is required.

Shokunin sharpen free-hand, and although there are commercially made sharpening jigs for *kanna* blades, I don't believe they give the same level of sharpness and quality of cutting edge that free-hand sharpening produces. Free-hand sharpening takes time to learn, but it is an important skill to master, and it will help you to maintain your *kanna* at its peak much more easily.

Posture

In the past *shokunin* in Japan were taught to sharpen squatting with their sharpening stones in a holder on the ground. Carpenters still sharpen this way. *Tateguya* and furniture makers, however, these days work at workbenches so they tend to sharpen while standing.

Relative to the head and shoulders, the position of the stone is the same regardless of whether the squatting or standing position is adopted for sharpening. Positioning the stone around navel height allows a relaxed stance with free arm and shoulder movement.

Hand and finger position

There is no single way of holding the blade for sharpening. Hand and finger sizes vary from person to person, so the way I hold the blade for sharpening may not necessarily be suitable for anyone else. The important thing is that the way you hold the blade is comfortable and relaxed,

and that there is even pressure along the width of the blade where it contacts the stone.

Angles and sharpening pattern

I sharpen the blade bevel at 25°–28°, and this gives me good results on both softwoods and hardwoods.

I angle the blade at 35°–45° to the stone, which provides solid support for the bevel so that it remains flat, and I sharpen with short strokes in three zones along the length of the stone. I also make sure I use the full width of the stone and not just the center to prevent it from dishing out in the middle.

By working in three zones on the stone, I can move my body forward and backward slightly as I shift zones so that my head remains in the same position relative to the blade, and this helps me avoid a scooping movement that would round the bevel.

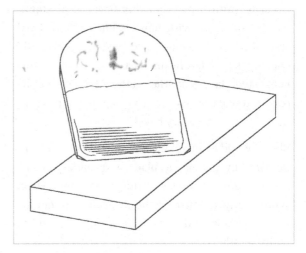

Diagram 36 Angle blade at 35°–45°

I do, however, have a tendency to place slightly more pressure on the right-hand or leading corner of the cutting edge when sharpening, resulting in a slight skew in the cutting edge if I'm not careful. I therefore examine the condition of the bevel often while sharpening so if faults such as this start to creep into my technique, I can correct them immediately.

The 70 mm *kanna* blade is heavier, thicker and wider than Western blades, and holding it stable on a sharpening stone can be quite awkward in the early stages. The weight of the blade tends to cause the *atama* to drop as you sharpen, leading to a rounded bevel or a slightly more acute bevel angle each time you sharpen.

Be aware of this, and by giving sufficient support to the *atama* as you sharpen, you will be able to avoid this and maintain a consistent bevel angle.

Secondary bevel?

A secondary bevel on Western plane blades is a convenient way of speeding up the sharpening process, especially considering that once the secondary bevel becomes too large after repeated rounds of sharpening, it's very easy to regrind the bevel on the grinder to bring it back to its original condition. This works well with Western plane blades, particularly when using a sharpening jig, but not so with the Japanese laminated blades.

Because of the thickness of Japanese blades, the bevel is quite broad, but this bevel is predominantly soft iron, with only a thin layer of hard steel at the cutting edge. A secondary bevel would encompass a significant part, if not all, of this hard steel layer, so the same effort would be required whether you are sharpening the primary bevel or the secondary bevel.

There would be virtually no reduction in sharpening time by giving the blade a secondary bevel, and the quality of the cutting edge would drop significantly because of the difficulty in keeping this narrow secondary bevel perfectly flat over its entire width.

A secondary bevel also has the risk of diminishing the cushioning effect of the soft iron on the hard steel when tapping out, with potentially disastrous and confidence-crushing results. My advice is therefore to take full advantage of the structure of the laminated blade, be patient and accept that sharpening cannot and must not be rushed, and learn to sharpen *kanna* blades free-hand with only a single bevel.

Back bevel?

The back bevel is also a convenient method of facilitating the sharpening process on Western plane blades. Western blades do not have an *urasuki*, so a much broader area back from the cutting edge has to be lapped and flattened when initially tuning the blade. After this initial tuning, a slight back bevel when polishing the back to remove the burr as the final step in sharpening reduces the area to polish, and also the time taken for sharpening.

A properly formed *ura* with an *ito-ura* (see Page 42), does not have as broad an area to keep flat. It is only the thin *uraba* and the two thin *ashi* that require polishing to remove the burr. So provided the *ura* is properly shaped with an *ito-ura*, essentially, all of the advantages and benefits of the back bevel for sharpening are inherent in the structure of the laminated Japanese blade.

So as long as you don't allow the *atama* to sag (see Page 45) when polishing the back to remove the burr, it is very simple to keep the thin *ito-ura* area flat, and a back bevel would simply be an additional and unnecessary step.

The second, although perhaps a less significant, reason to avoid a back bevel on Japanese blades is that the chip-breaker should be set back 0.1–0.2 mm from the blade cutting edge on the *shiage-kanna* and about 0.2 mm on the *chū-shikō kanna* (see Diagram 9 on Page 12, and Page 15), and a back bevel presents a slight risk of interfering with the contact between the *uraba* and the chip-breaker.

A back bevel is also an effective way of increasing the cutting angle for planing hardwood with a difficult grain pattern. In this case I would still avoid a back bevel on the *kanna* blade, and instead use a *kanna* with a higher bedding and cutting angle, or use a Western plane that has a blade with a suitable back bevel.

MAINTENANCE

Unlike metal Western planes, *kanna* require regular maintenance of the *dai* and blade assembly to keep functioning at their best. Here I'll cover this in two sections; maintenance of the *dai*, and maintenance of the blade, including the chip-breaker.

Dai

A highly tuned *kanna* that's working well in the morning can turn into an absolute beast that's impossible to use in the afternoon. Or it can feel like a completely different plane when a clear sunny day becomes overcast and rain starts to fall. In extreme cases, it can even stop working altogether while you are actually in the middle of using it.

This is one of the characteristics of *kanna*, and one that can often reinforce in Western woodworkers' minds the myth that *kanna* are temperamental tools that are just too difficult. In reality, though, the solution is very simple, and need only take a few minutes on a regular basis.

As you are well aware, wood is affected by the weather, and the level of humidity in the surrounding area, and this is no different for the *dai*. Any movement by the *dai* because of the weather must be corrected otherwise the *kanna* ceases to function properly, or even at all.

As soon as you start to sense any change in how the *kanna* feels or responds, stop planing and carry out the following maintenance.

This is generally the same process I described in conditioning the sole for a new *kanna* from Page 31.

(1)   Retract the blade and chip-breaker about 1–2 mm from the mouth.

(2)   Check the sole with your straightedge against the light in the order described in Diagram 32 on Page 32. What you are looking for here is if there are any points outside the three (or two) contact surfaces where the sole touches the straightedge; whether the contact surface near the blade is flat all the way across; and whether there is any twist over the length of the *dai*.

(3)   If the straightedge contacts the sole at any point in either of the two recessed parts between the contact surfaces, these elevated points are raising the cutting edge off the planing surface so all you need to do is lightly scrape across the sole to remove these elevations with the *dainaoshi kanna* (or cabinet scraper). This is the simplest problem to rectify. Check the sole again with the straightedge, and if the elevated points have been properly removed and there are no other problems, you've finished and you can continue planing.

(4)   If the *tsutsumi* area on the *dai-gashira* side of the mouth has warped and this is raising the cutting edge off the planing surface (see Diagram 35 on Page 34) use a sharp chisel to scrape away the elevated point, taking care not to scratch the blade or remove any material from the contact surface near the mouth.

(5)   If you have three contact surfaces and the straightedge does not have even contact with all three, i.e. one of the contact surfaces is either lower or higher than the other two at any point across the width, or if the contact surface at the mouth is not perfectly flat across its entire width, slightly more work is necessary. What you will need to do in these cases is to flatten the sole with 220–240 grit sandpaper as explained in the section on conditioning the sole. The sole has already been conditioned, so this should take no more than a few backward and forward movements on the sandpaper, depending on how badly the *dai* has warped.

(6)   Scrape away the recessed areas between the three contact surfaces with the *dainaoshi kanna* and the chisel exactly as you did

during the initial conditioning of the sole, and don't forget to check the sides of the mouth. If necessary, pare away a small amount of wood to create the recess both sides of the mouth as well.

(7)   Check the sole again with the straightedge, and if all seems well, do a test cut to confirm the problem has been rectified, and continue planing.

You may need to carry out maintenance on your *kanna* every day or every couple of days, or it may not need any maintenance for a week or so. Regardless of the frequency, these simple steps will keep your *kanna dai* in top condition, and should take no more than a few minutes to complete. As you become more accustomed to using *kanna*, you will very quickly develop a feel for what is causing any problem, and this will further reduce the time taken for *dai* maintenance.

Blade

You've been using your *kanna* for a while and have kept it well maintained so it gives you the thinnest and most satisfying shavings you could imagine. To make sure you keep getting those wonderful translucent shavings, you've been sharpening the blade regularly and with an abundance of care to avoid all the bad habits and poor techniques that could create planing frustration.

You have noticed, though, that over time the hollow (*urasuki*) has gradually moved its way closer to the cutting edge, and after a couple of more rounds on the sharpening stones, the *urasuki* will reach the edge. This is known as *uragire*. What do you do when the flat area (*uraba*) becomes too narrow, or vanishes completely?

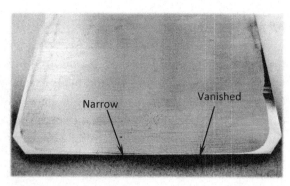

Photograph 24 *Uragire*

What you have to do now is a two-part procedure that can be quite terrifying — *ura-dashi* (tapping out) and *ura-oshi* (flattening the back). If not done properly, the first part — tapping out — has the potential to permanently ruin your expensive blade, and the second part — *ura-oshi* — has the potential to cause many years of embarrassment.

The first part in particular is a procedure that woodworkers new to *kanna* dread and try to avoid, but in reality, with the right amount of care, it is no more difficult than carrying out normal maintenance on your *dai*.

Tapping out (ura-dashi)

Why do we have to tap out? If it's such a risky procedure why don't we just keep flattening the back until the *uraba* is broad enough so we don't need to tap out?

A broad *uraba*, and wide *ashi* to the sides of the *urasuki* is certainly an ugly sight to see, but it goes well beyond the aesthetics. A blade is sharp when two flat and highly polished edges join. That's why in the initial setting-up process we have to be so particular about flattening and polishing the back.

As we sharpen the bevel, we create a burr on the back, and provided the back is properly flattened and polished, we only need to stroke it a few times on our finishing stone to remove the burr for a sharp edge. There's no need to put the back through the different grits of stone as we sharpen the bevel. That's one of the first points we learn when we begin to sharpen.

The *urasuki* in the *ura* helps to stabilize the blade on the finishing stone by reducing the overall area of contact, and this in turn makes it easier to achieve good contact between the blade edge and the stone and to remove the burr for a sharp cutting edge. The narrower the flat area to the front and sides of the *urasuki*, the more efficient this polishing and burr removal is, and the easier it is to keep the back perfectly flat.

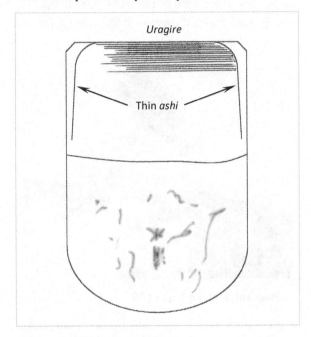

Diagram 37 Tapping out 01

If we fail to tap out when our sharpening has brought us to the *uragire* condition, or we don't tap out properly or sufficiently, we're creating two problems, one of which is very serious indeed.

If we don't tap out or don't tap out enough, we need to remove a substantial amount of very hard metal from the two *ashi* to form a reasonable *uraba* again that we can polish and keep flat (Diagram 38).

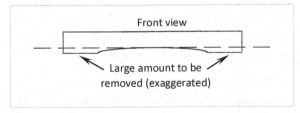

Diagram 38 Tapping out 02

In the process, though, we've created two fat *ashi*, and more than likely a lopsided *uraba*. As we've increased the flat area and the area we have to keep flat, we've made it more difficult to achieve good contact between the blade edge and the stone and to remove the burr.

If we again fail to tap out or tap out properly the next time the blade reaches an *uragire* condition, we will need to remove even more hard steel from the *ashi* to recreate our flat *uraba*. This will make the *ashi* even fatter, make our lopsided *uraba* even more lopsided and wider, and cause the sharpening process to become even more difficult, time-consuming and frustrating.

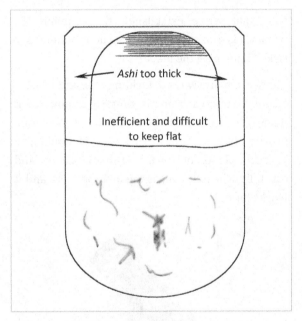

Diagram 39 Tapping out 03

As bad as this is, the second problem is even more serious. *Kanna* blades are wedge-shaped, and it's this wedge shape that seats the blade firmly in the *dai*. That's why in the initial setting up process, we flattened the back of the blade first, then adjusted the *omote-najimi* and *osae-mizo* in the *dai* so the blade fits securely.

In other words, when flattening the back, we established the thickness of the blade and the wedge shape near the cutting edge, then adjusted the *dai* relative to this.

If we were to remove the necessary amount of material from the sides to recreate the *uraba* from an *uragire* condition without tapping out, and repeated this several times, we would have radically altered the thickness of the blade and therefore the geometry of the wedge. The blade would be extremely loose in the *dai*, and the cutting edge would simply drop through the mouth.

In this state, the *kanna* is unusable. To fix this, we would need to insert a paper shim on the *omote-najimi* to secure the blade more firmly, but the value in this is questionable because if we still fail to tap out properly, we will continue aggravating the problem until it becomes no longer possible to shim the blade, and the *kanna* is ruined.

Now that we've established that tapping out properly is essential, how do we do it without the risk of damaging the blade?

There are many ways of tackling this, and provided they work, each one is as good as any other. Regardless of the method you use, this is one process that must not be rushed. You should give yourself plenty of time, and work slowly and carefully. The following is the method I use, and it works for me.

Photograph 25 Tapping out 04

I use a corner of my workbench that I've rounded off with a file to give good support to the *urasuki*. Any firm surface can be used provided it gives solid support. Small anvils, and even short cut-offs of railway track are used in Japan. My workbench is Queensland maple, which is a reasonably firm Australian hardwood. I've also filed the vertical edge to give my forefinger a flat reference point.

I tap out using the bottom edge of a 185 gram *gennō*. Photograph 25 shows how I rest the blade on the corner of the workbench so that it gives full support. The key here is to ensure that the blade is always supported at the striking point, so move the blade rather than the *gennō*; that is, always strike with the *gennō* at the same point.

Photograph 26 Tapping out 05

A good indication of how hard you should strike the blade is to imagine yourself tapping a very thin nail into a piece of wood, and the nail entry must be perfectly vertical without any bending or deviation. This is the force and the control you should use — many light taps rather than a few hefty smashes. The latter will almost guarantee a crack or a chip. A chip, or a crack in the hard steel that runs across the blade can be repaired, but a crack that runs up the length of the blade cannot, and the blade is completely ruined.

Where to strike with the *gennō* will be determined by the shape of the *uragire* — tapping should be slightly more concentrated in the area where the *uraba* has vanished, and less so in the areas where a small *uraba* remains.

In Photograph 24 on Page 38 you will notice that the *uraba* has vanished on the right-hand side, but remains, although very narrow, on the left-hand side. Slightly more tapping should be done on the side with no *uraba*. Where the *uragire* is consistent across the cutting edge, the tapping should be evenly distributed. The important point here, and one that I continually emphasize, is that you must always examine the blade, because it will let you know the areas you need to work on.

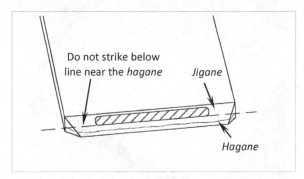

Diagram 40 Tapping out 06

You should aim at a distribution of tap marks over the back half of the bevel covering about three-quarters of the width. You should not strike near the *mimi*, and you should definitely not strike near the hard steel cutting edge (*hagane*).

I check the *ura* regularly with a small straight-edge as I tap out to gauge my progress. As a bulge begins to form in the *urasuki*, I can determine whether I need to tap more or less in any area. When I think I've achieved an even bulge in the *urasuki*, I stroke the *ura* lightly on my 2000 grit sharpening stone a couple of times where I've tapped out and check the scratch pattern.

If the scratches from the stone are more to one side than the other, I know that I need to tap some more on the side without the scratches. If there is a scratch pattern to the sides but nothing in the middle, I need to tap out more in the middle area. What I'm hoping to see are even scratches in the middle, fading away to nothing well before the sides, and I continue tapping out until I achieve this. This is essentially the same as when tuning a new blade.

The *ura* will very quickly tell you whether your tapping is too strong in one area, or isn't properly distributed, and also any other technical faults you have. The telltale signs are covered in detail in the *Ito-ura* section from Page 42.

Flattening the back (ura-oshi)

Flattening the back after tapping out is in some respects similar to the initial flattening process I described in Adjusting a new plane from Page 25. However, because the condition of the blade, and especially the back, is considerably different, there are pitfalls that you need to be aware of to avoid long-term embarrassment.

When flattening the back of a new blade, with a quality blade and under normal circumstances you should only have to remove a fairly small amount of steel to get it flat, and for all subsequent sharpening sessions, you should only ever use the fine grit stone on the back just to remove the burr. So any faults you may have in your back honing technique probably won't show up to any noticeable degree. Flattening after tapping out is another matter altogether.

When tapping out, we create a bulge in the *urasuki* near the cutting edge, and it's this bulge that we have to hone away to flatten the back. We therefore have to remove considerably more material than in the initial flattening process, so poor technique here will show up to a much greater degree.

In this section I'll briefly cover the process I use to flatten after tapping out, then I'll discuss in somewhat more detail the kind of *ura* you should be aiming at, how to achieve it, and some of the problems you should avoid.

(1)   When the 2000 grit stone leaves an even scratch pattern in the middle of the *urasuki* near the cutting edge indicating I have tapped out successfully and sufficiently, I move to the 1000 grit stone. I carefully hone the end 10–15 mm of the *ura*, moving the blade left and right on the stone while at the same time moving it forward and backward 10–20 mm so a ridge doesn't form. At the same time, I make sure the blade *atama* doesn't sag as I hone. At this stage, the *uraba* has formed, and as soon as there is an even scratch pattern across the entire width of the newly formed *uraba*, I move to the 2000 grit stone. This is the

point that needs to be stressed. As soon as the scratches extend fully across the entire width, stop immediately, and move on to the next finer stone.

(2)   From here, I'm simply removing the scratches and polishing the back as I progress through the 2000, 5000, and 8000 grit stones (or to the 12000 stone for my finishing planes). Again, continue with each grit only until the scratches of the previous stone have been fully removed and replaced by the finer scratches of the current stone.

(3)   The geometry of the back has been changed slightly because of the tapping out, so I also check the contact between the blade and the chip-breaker, and make any necessary adjustments to the chip-breaker in exactly the same way that was done during the initial adjustment described from Page 29.

From here, its on to the normal sharpening process. The marks made in the bevel by the *gennō* when tapping out have no effect on the performance of the blade, and will disappear after two or three sharpening sessions.

Ito-ura

Shokunin in Japan are very particular about how the blade *ura* looks. It can be a source of pride, or it can cause shame and embarrassment. A properly shaped *ura* not only makes the blade and the *kanna* more efficient, but is also a testament to the *shokunin's* skill and his respect for his tools. A badly shaped *ura* shows a lack of care that is more than likely to be carried through to the *shokunin's* work.

In this section, I'll describe in detail how to create and maintain an *ura* you can be proud of, and how to avoid the bad habits that will prevent you from achieving this.

The type of *ura* to aim at is an *ito-ura*.

Photograph 27 *Ito-ura*

Ito is the Japanese word for thread, and in an *ito-ura* the *uraba* is as thin as a thread, or in reality about 1–2 mm. The hard steel and soft iron lamination structure of a *kanna* blade is different from that of a chisel, so they have different *ura*, as shown in Photograph 28. The chisel *ura* is broader, and is known as *beta-ura*. A reasonable *beta-ura* is normal on a chisel, but not on a *kanna* blade. This is the type of *ura* you should avoid.

Photograph 28 *Ito-ura* and *beta-ura*

There are a number of faults that can create a badly formed *ura*, but the advantage is that they all affect the *ura* in a different way so if you are having difficulties in obtaining or keeping a good *ito-ura*, the *ura* itself will tell you where the problem is.

The main faults are: a failure to tap out adequately, and closely linked to this, honing the back too much, especially on the coarser grits; an uneven distribution of strikes when tapping out; honing along a single line; honing at an angle not perpendicular to the stone; and, perhaps the most common, allowing the blade *atama* to sag while honing.

Failure to tap out adequately

This can be a common problem when tapping out from the *uragire* condition, but it can also occur if you don't properly tap out a new blade that has a slight elevation at a point along the cutting edge. This aspect was covered in the Adjusting a new plane section beginning on Page 25.

The following diagram shows what happens when the tapping out is inadequate. This can often be caused by a degree of tentativeness when tapping out, especially in the early stages. Although not as bad a problem as not tapping out at all (see Page 39), over time the problem will continue to worsen.

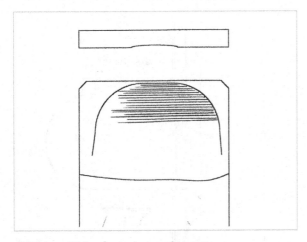

Diagram 41 Inadequate tapping out

The way to solve this is very simple indeed. If, after tapping out, you hone the *ura* on the coarse stone and the scratch patterns reach both sides of the blade but the *uraba* has not widened sufficiently or not at all, STOP. Don't try to force out the *uraba* on the stone.

If you continue honing until a reasonable *uraba* appears, you will hone too much, and while you may end up with a thin *uraba*, the *ashi* on both sides will be too thick. Once this happens you are virtually stuck with fat *ashi* for the rest of the life of the blade.

This is also the case if you don't tap out adequately on a new blade. If you've tapped out adequately but hone too much on the coarser stone, you will end up with a *beta-ura*.

Tapping out must be a careful and deliberate procedure, but that does not mean you should be tentative. Tap, check, tap, check, and continue until a sufficient bulge appears, regardless of how long it takes.

Uneven tap distribution

In this case, tapping has been concentrated too much in one area so the bulge in the *urasuki* isn't uniform. The following diagrams show what happens when the tapping is not even.

(1)   Tapping too much or too strongly in the center and not enough on the sides: This can be a tendency in the early stages, where the center seems the safest.

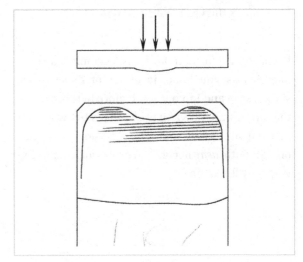

Diagram 42 Uneven tap distribution 01

(2)   Tapping too much or too strongly to one side: This quite often happens if the *uragire* is more to one side, and you fail to account for it .

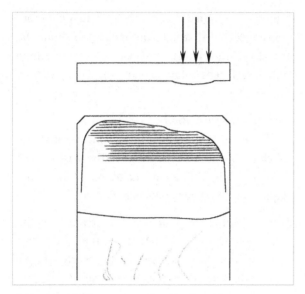

Diagram 43 Uneven tap distribution 02

If you find that your *uraba* is beginning to look like this as you hone, in either of these cases, simply stop and tap out some more in those areas that are too shallow. An *uraba* that's too wide can be fixed after a few sharpening sessions, but once one or both *ashi* become overly wide, that's the way they'll remain.

Honing along a single line

If you hone the *ura* along a single line on the sharpening stones you will create a ridge, which is another sign of poor technique. Therefore as you hone the blade along the stone, especially the coarser grit stones after tapping out, gradually move it backward and forward 10–20 mm to prevent the ridge from forming.

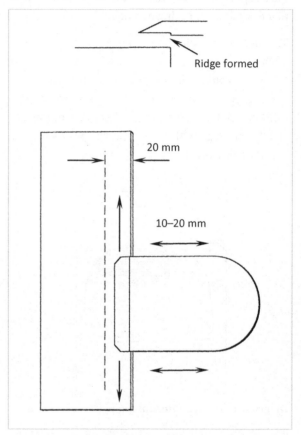

Ridge formed

20 mm

10–20 mm

Diagram 44 Avoid forming a ridge in the blade

44

Honing at an angle

When honing the *ura*, the blade should be perpendicular to the length of the stone. If the blade is at an angle you run the risk of an *ura* that looks like the following.

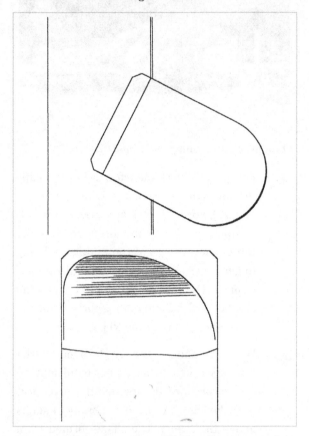

Diagram 45 Poor *ura* caused by honing at an angle

Sagging atama while honing

This is perhaps the most commonly seen fault. *Kanna* blades are quite large and heavy, and there is a tendency to let the *atama* sag while honing the *back*, giving the *ura* somewhat of an hourglass shape. The following diagrams show this.

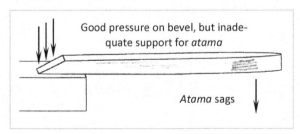

Good pressure on bevel, but inadequate support for *atama*

Atama sags

Diagram 46 Poor support for *atama*

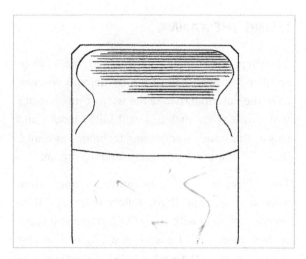

Diagram 47 Hourglass-shaped *ura*

When honing the back, you should have a feeling that you're lifting the *atama* up slightly with your supporting hand as you apply pressure to the bevel with your other hand.

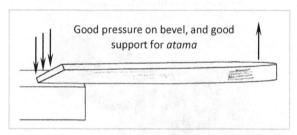

Good pressure on bevel, and good support for *atama*

Diagram 48 Good support for *atama*

You shouldn't actually raise the *atama* as this would give you an unwanted back-bevel, just feel as though you are. That way you are giving the blade proper and even support, and you'll avoid the hourglass shape. Unfortunately, once you have the hourglass *ura*, you're stuck with it until you're able to sharpen past it, which could take several years.

Using the Kanna

Adjusting and tuning the *dai* and blade/chip-breaker has been half of the battle, and we now have the potential to take the wispy thin shavings that can leave a surface beautifully smooth and glossy. But unless our planing technique is sound, those shavings will only ever remain a dream.

The following is a list of points to note when using a *kanna*, and if you follow them, and with practice, planing with the pulling action will begin to feel more natural and you'll notice a vast improvement in the quality of the planed surface.

(1) The workpiece should be at about the same height as the bottom of your hipbone. Any higher, and your arms and shoulders become cramped; any lower, and you have to stoop over too much to reach.

Photograph 29 Planing technique 01

(2) If you're right-handed, the right hand should be positioned midway between the *kōana* and the *dai-jiri* with the fingers wrapped over the *dai* naturally. The sides of the *dai* are held firmly by the thumb on the left side and the middle and ring fingers on the right. The forefinger rests naturally along the chamfered edge of the *uwaba* next to the corner of the *kōana* to keep the *dai* balanced. The front of the palm is raised off the *dai*, and this levers the back of the palm to hold the *dai-jiri* down firmly.

Photograph 30 Planing technique 02

(3) For general work the left hand lightly cups the top half of the blade (Photographs 30 and 32). For fine work or work on narrower stock, the thumb and forefinger hold the top of the blade, and the middle and ring fingers rest on and wrap around the *dai-gashira*. The little finger doesn't touch the *dai*, but slides lightly along the side of the workpiece (Photograph 31).

(4) When planing, the right-hand wrist remains relaxed, the plane, hand and elbow form a straight line, and the lower arm is tucked in. The head generally remains above the *kanna*. The shape formed from the elbow through to the *kanna* should remain constant throughout the planing motion.

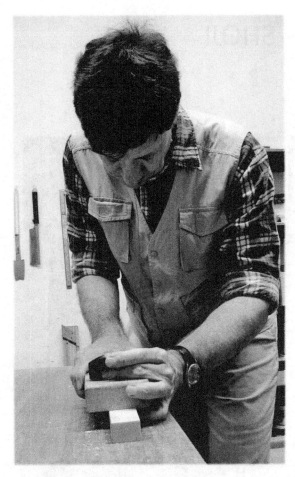

Photograph 31 Planing technique 03

(5) Planing is done with the hips and the entire upper body, not just the arms and shoulders. On longer workpieces the legs move to form a comfortable stance, then the hips and shoulders move in unison to pull the *kanna* smoothly along. These are two distinct movements, but should be done in one smooth continual motion.

(6) On shorter workpieces, the legs adopt a comfortable stance, and the hips pull the upper body back, drawing the *kanna* smoothly along the workpiece surface. If you use just your arms to pull the *kanna*, it is impossible to maintain firm and consistent pressure, resulting in a surface that is neither flat nor square.

(7) As is the case with Western planes as well, the *kanna* should not be lifted from the surface midway through the planing stroke.

Photograph 32 Planing technique 04

PART 2 — SHOJI

Photograph 33 *Fukiyose-shōji* with *ennuki-shōji* on top

BRIEF HISTORY OF SHOJI

To gain a better appreciation of how to make shoji and how best to adapt them to our individual needs and situation, we need to understand how and why they originated, and how they evolved into the style we know today.

To trace the origins of shoji, we have to head back in Japanese history to the Nara Period (710-794), or even before that to the Asuka Period (574-710).

The Hōryū-ji Temple grounds in Nara Prefecture contain some of the oldest wooden structures existing in the world. The original temple, commissioned by Prince Shōtoku (574-622), is thought to have been completed in about 607, but was later destroyed by fire, and rebuilt in 711.

One of the buildings within the complex is the Denpōdō. Ancient records regarding the Denpōdō from the Nara Period mention walls, doors, and hanging cloth screens (*kichō*) and wooden screens partitioning the large open internal space of the building, but they also mention screen-like partitions with a timber *kumiko* lattice on to which silk cloth was affixed on both sides. This is perhaps the first historical mention of a partitioning system that resembles the modern-day opaque *fusuma* doors and dividers.

Photograph 34 Denpōdō, Nara

The Heian Period (794-1185) saw the introduction of the *shinden-zukuri* architectural style for aristocratic mansions. At the core of this was the *moya*, a large open-spaced room for entertaining and ceremonies that could be divided easily and flexibly through the use of increasingly elaborate screens and partitions. Silk-covered *fusuma* therefore became much more widely used. The famous Heian Period novel *Tale of Genji* also mentioned *fusuma* that could "open and close", so we know that by this time double-sliding *fusuma* partitions had made their appearance in the homes of the Court nobles.

Patterned paper from China (*karakami*) also made its way to Japan, and began to be used on *fusuma*, along with the more traditional silk covering. These types of *fusuma* were referred to as *fusuma-shōji* and *karakami-shōji*.

Japan had introduced paper manufacturing techniques from China in the seventh century, but with major advances in this technology in the late Heian Period, paper-makers now had the skills to manufacture thin translucent paper. When this paper was attached to wooden frames and these frames were fitted as partitions in rooms, the paper allowed an even diffusion of light in the room, but could restrict wind and glare. This was the birth of the shoji we know today.

To differentiate these from the existing *fusuma*, this new fitting was called *akari-shōji* (*akari* is the Japanese word for light). Over time, the *akari* part was dropped, as was the shoji part of *fusuma*, so the opaque silk or *karakami* partitions were known simply as *fusuma*, and the paper-backed partitions were referred to simply as shoji. These terms have continued through to the present day.

Later during the Kamakura (1185-1333) and Muromachi (1333-1573) Periods the household living space evolved with the introduction of covered ceilings and the greater use of tatami throughout the residence, so sliding *fusuma* and shoji fitted between structural pillars were used extensively to partition rooms.

Forming a backdrop to this was the gradual transition of political power from the court nobles to the samurai warrior class, and over time the general function of the residence changed into more of a focus on the reception of guests.

These social gatherings among the samurai and noble elite steadily took on greater political significance and importance, and became a central part of everyday life. Poetry, flower arrangement, the tea ceremony and other arts flourished, sweeping landscapes were painted on *fusuma*, and more complex shoji patterns were adopted as rooms became more elaborately decorated.

During the Momoyama Period (1573-1603), the samurai class continued to grow more powerful, and *shoin-zukuri*, perhaps Japan's most important residential architectural style and one that has had a major influence on traditional Japanese building construction right through to the modern day, became firmly established.

Photograph 35 *Tokonoma* **with** *shoin-shōji* **and** *ranma* **(transom)**

Shoin-zukuri, which incorporated a formal reception area of two or three tatami rooms partitioned by various kinds of sliding doors, and a decorative alcove (*tokonoma*) in the main reception room, took shoji to a new level of elegance, especially through the *shoin-shōji* covering windows in the main reception room.

In the four centuries since then, shoji design has continued to be refined, and has risen to new heights of complexity and artistic expression with the advent of modern materials, tools and techniques.

The greater use of computers and the enhanced accuracy afforded by computer-controlled cutters has also seen kumiko art — *kumiko-zaiku* — reach new levels, and boundaries are being pushed with every generation.

Notwithstanding the many advances in modern technology, the hand skills of the *tateguya* and kumiko *shokunin*, though, are paramount, and the bulk of their work is still done by hand using techniques passed down from one generation to the next.

TYPES AND CHARACTERISTICS

Shoji are broadly classified both by kumiko arrangement and by structure, and all shoji are a combination of both. Although there was a functional consideration for kumiko arrangement in the past in terms of dimensions of the shoji paper, these days with modern commercially manufactured shoji paper, decisions are largely based on aesthetics, and of course, cost. Shoji structure, though, is primarily functional.

Shoji anatomy

The following is a diagram of the first shoji we'll make listing all the part names.

For all shoji I'll use the English names where an equivalent exists, such as rails, stiles, and horns. 'Kumiko' is the standard term in English for the lattice pieces, and 'tsukeko' is the only suitable thing to call the internal frame pieces between the main frame and the kumiko without groping for an English word.

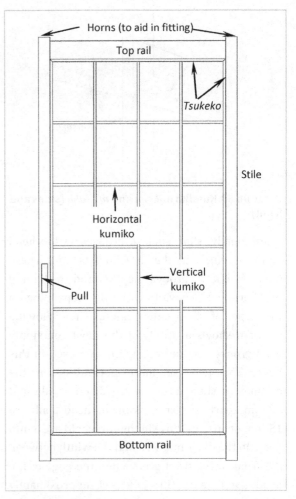

Diagram 49 Shoji anatomy

One set of Japanese terms I will use throughout the book, though, is *mitsuke* and *mikomi*. As shown in the following diagram, *mitsuke* is the front of the kumiko that can be seen when looking straight at the shoji, and *mikomi* is the side of the kumiko. These are convenient terms that prevent any confusion that may arise using 'thickness', 'depth', 'width' and any other similar word, so I'll use these and only these to indicate the front or sides of the kumiko.

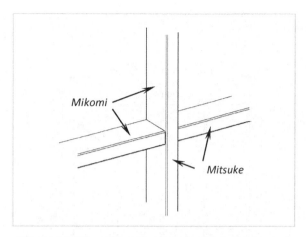

Diagram 50 Kumiko *mikomi* and *mitsuke* (sides and front)

Traditionally, shoji slide in grooves in the head jamb (*kamoi*) and the threshold (*shikii*). These have standard groove depths and a limited number of groove width variations depending on the type of shoji and region. The following diagram shows a profile of the most commonly used groove set, and this is the one used in this book. The two (or more depending on the number of shoji) grooves are 21 mm wide and 12 mm apart. The grooves in the head jamb are 15 mm deep, and those in the threshold are 3 mm deep. In the diagram I've listed the width between the front of the front groove and the edge of the head jamb and threshold as approximately 15 mm, but this can be any width as long as the shoji does not overhang the edges. Rebates are cut in the top and bottom of the shoji to run in these grooves. In this book I'll cover the variations for top rails and rebates, not just the traditional style, so you can have further choices on how your shoji will look.

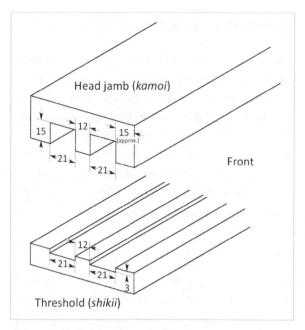

Diagram 51 Grooves for shoji

Kumiko arrangement

In the past, before the introduction of modern paper manufacturing technology, kumiko arrangement was determined by the width of the *washi* (Japanese hand-made paper). The standard shoji with total dimensions of just under 1,800 x 900 mm could contain a minimum of five horizontal kumiko, and for balance, three vertical kumiko. This ratio of three : five kumiko, or four : six equal intervals became the traditional kumiko arrangement, and even today with modern paper and none of the width limitations of the past, this ratio still forms the foundation of kumiko design (see Diagram 52 on Page 54).

This traditional arrangement of three vertical and five horizontal kumiko is known as ***aragumi-shōji*** (or *arama-shōji*), and the light and subtle atmosphere that it conveys makes it a popular style of shoji in tea ceremony houses. It has also become extensively used in Japanese homes today, especially considering it is the least time-consuming and therefore the least costly of the kumiko arrangements. This is the first of the shoji we make in this book.

The *yokogumi-shōji* is simply the standard horizontal kumiko arrangement with an additional horizontal kumiko dividing each vertical interval — 11 horizontal kumiko giving 12 equal intervals. This has been a popular shoji design since the beginning, and is regarded as ideally suited to the traditional Japanese living space, particularly open sub-dividable Japanese-style rooms.

If we add another kumiko into each of the intervals, we have what is known as the *yokoshige-shōji*. There are now 23 horizontal kumiko dividing the vertical space into 24 equal intervals. Removing the outer two vertical kumiko and leaving just the center one for much wider horizontal intervals has a very elegant feel, and is often used in areas with expansive wall space. Of course, there are countless variations on these and all the other kumiko arrangements, but this gives an idea of how all the designs essentially stem from the traditional kumiko arrangement.

If we increase the vertical kumiko to five or seven to split the horizontal dimension into six or eight equal parts, and keep the five horizontal kumiko in the standard arrangement, the intervals are now vertically elongated, and this design is the very stylish *tategumi-shōji*. If we add even more vertical kumiko to make the intervals even narrower, the design becomes *tateshige-shōji*. It is also called *yanagi-shōji*, or "willow shoji", which is a very apt and charmingly descriptive name for this design. The *tateshige* design is often used in formal Japanese-style drawing rooms next to the *tokonoma*.

The arrangement with a large number of both horizontal and vertical kumiko is called *honshige-shōji*, and if the kumiko are not made narrower than they are in the other kinds of shoji,

this pattern can look somewhat heavy, or even oppressive. In *masugumi-shōji* the vertical and horizontal kumiko intervals are as near to the same as possible so that the kumiko form squares. This is a fairly neutral design, so it can be seen in both Japanese-style and Western-style homes or rooms.

In all the above examples, the kumiko are spaced at even intervals, but another very attractive design is created by arranging the kumiko in groups, either vertically or horizontally, or both. *Fukiyose-shōji* breaks the uniform rhythm of kumiko arrangement in an effort to avoid monotony, and the subtle balances this design can achieve and the mild informality it expresses are its primary appeal. Kumiko can be grouped in any reasonable number — two or three is the most popular — and the spacing can vary between groups and also between kumiko within groups, but balance is the critical factor when designing this arrangement.

These are examples of the standard kumiko arrangements, but the number of both vertical and horizontal for each can vary, and you will probably need to make adjustments depending on the size of the shoji you are making. The important aspect, though, is to make sure you have the correct balance. Making the kumiko *mitsuke* slightly narrower on shoji with a large number of kumiko, and slightly wider on those with fewer kumiko is a good start to achieving a pleasing balance.

These standard arrangements also form the basis for many other more complex patterns. We touch on a couple of these slightly more advanced arrangements in the second and third shoji we make — the *kasumi-gumi*, and the *kawari-gumi*.

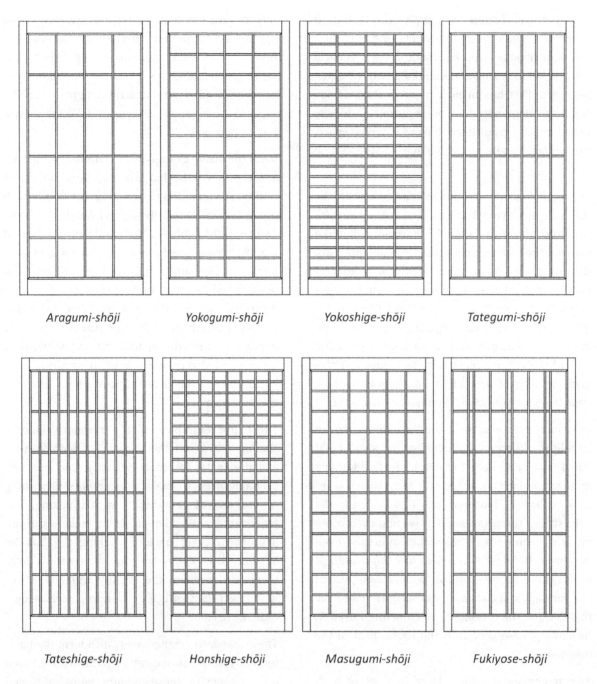

| Aragumi-shōji | Yokogumi-shōji | Yokoshige-shōji | Tategumi-shōji |

| Tateshige-shōji | Honshige-shōji | Masugumi-shōji | Fukiyose-shōji |

Diagram 52 Types of kumiko arrangement

Structure

This is the functional classification of shoji, and many forms have been developed over the centuries to meet a range of functional needs. At the basic structural level, the two kinds of shoji are ***mizugoshi-shōji***, which is the simplest of all structures and consists of the frame and kumiko assembly (all of the examples in Diagram 52 are mizugoshi-shōji), and ***koshitsuki-shōji***, which is fitted with a hip-board at the bottom. *Koshitsuki-shōji* are somewhat of a relic from the era when shoji were used for external doors and windows, and the panel was attached to protect the shoji paper against the elements. The panels in the earliest shoji were therefore quite high (*koshida-ka-shōji*), in some cases accounting for almost half the size of the shoji, but the panel height steadily fell as shoji came to be used more as an internal fixture. Until the beginning of WWII *koshitsuki-shōji* were the norm, but these days most shoji installed in homes are *mizugoshi-shōji*, although in very formal Japanese-style drawing rooms *koshitsuki-shōji* are still popular because they tend to convey an atmosphere of calmness and tranquility. *Mizugoshi-shōji*, on the other hand, are ideal for the less formal daily living space where the inherent lightness of this type of shoji is preferred.

The garden has always been a key feature of traditional Japanese homes, and the **suriage-shōji** was developed to allow the garden to be viewed while the shoji are closed. This type of shoji has a range of names, including *yukimi-shōji*, which means 'snow-viewing shoji' and is the most commonly used term, *suriage-nekoma*, and *ōsaka-nekoma*. It consists of a small moveable shoji frame on the bottom called *ko-shōji* that is offset from the fixed shoji frame on top and can be raised or lowered in grooves. These days behind the *ko-shōji* when it is closed is a fixed glass panel. This type can have a *mizugoshi* or *koshitsuki* structure, and is common throughout Japan.

Gakuiri-shōji are shoji that contain a glass frame within the kumiko assembly. The types of *gakuiri-shōji* are based on the size or orientation of the glass frame: **jikagarasu-shōji** (also called *ōgakuiri-shōji*) features a large glass frame at the bottom of the shoji or directly above the hip-board; **tategakuiri-shōji** contains a rectangular glass frame with a vertical orientation; and **yokogakuiri-shōji** has a glass frame with a horizontal orientation.

Shoji with *ko-shōji* that slide in grooves horizontally rather than vertically as in the *suriage-shōji* are called **nekoma-shōji**, and these are further broken down into **katabiki-nekoma**, which consists of a single *ko-shōji* and therefore the opening is either on the right or left; **hikiwake-nekoma**, which has two small *ko-shōji* that open up either side so the opening is in the center, and **hikichigai-nekoma**, which has two *ko-shōji* that slide the entire width. The frame structure and sliding mechanism of the *ko-shōji* in this kind of shoji are different from those in the *suriage-shōji*. In the early stages these weren't fitted with glass panels, but these days most are; the *hikichigai-nekoma* shoji, though, doesn't have a glass panel.

These are the basic shoji structures that are widely used today. A simple change in the kumiko arrangement or in the size or orientation of a glass panel, or the addition of a hip-board can alter the feeling and sense of quality a shoji conveys quite dramatically.

All of the various kumiko arrangements I covered briefly in the previous section can be used with each of the functional structures I describe above, so you can see that the range of design options is virtually limitless.

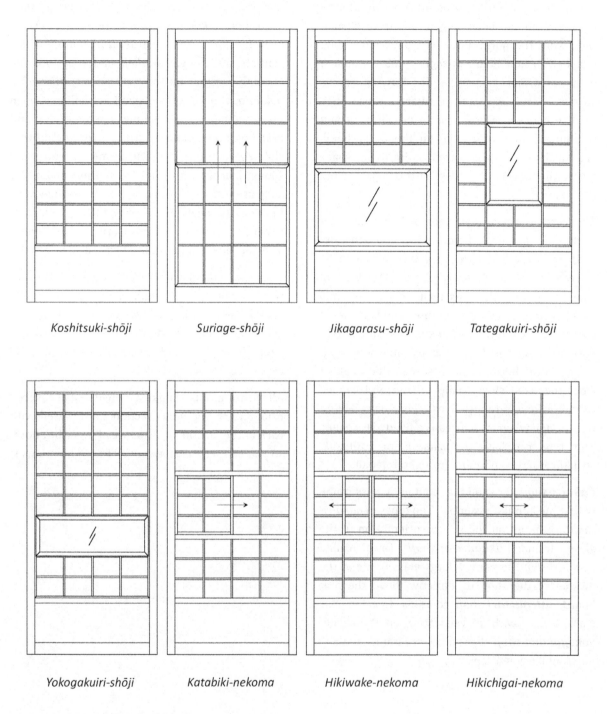

Koshitsuki-shōji   Suriage-shōji   Jikagarasu-shōji   Tategakuiri-shōji

Yokogakuiri-shōji   Katabiki-nekoma   Hikiwake-nekoma   Hikichigai-nekoma

Diagram 53 Types of shoji structure

MAKING A STANDARD SHOJI

Photograph 36 *Mizugoshi* **shoji**

In this section I'll explain how to make a pair of standard shoji with an *aragumi* kumiko arrangement and a *mizugoshi* structure. The overall dimensions I use for the shoji itself equate to a scaled down version of a standard set of doors, but these can of course be adjusted as required. I'll therefore give clear instructions on how to calculate the size of shoji according to the size of the opening, and also the interval between individual kumiko so that you can alter the sizes according to your own needs, but still maintain the same kumiko pattern and feel. In cases where I feel adjustments need to be made to the kumiko to retain a sense of balance in a larger or smaller shoji, I'll mention these specifically.

From this shoji and using the following procedures, it's a very simple matter to take the next step and design your own kumiko arrangement.

Other than initial timber dimensioning, almost all processes will be done by hand, and I've listed the tools and jigs you'll find necessary to make the shoji. If additional jigs or tools are required for a particular type of shoji or kumiko pattern, I will list them in the relevant section.

Japanese tools are not essential for making shoji, and if you have good quality Western tools, there's no need to go out and buy a complete set of their Japanese counterparts, although there are a couple that will make the process much easier. I've marked these with an asterisk.

Tools

Layout

(1) Straightedge

(2) Metal try square — For 90° marking; must be solid and accurate

(3) Large try square

(4) Miter square — For 45° marking; must be solid and accurate

(5) Marking knife

(6) Marking gauge (or the marking gauge jig shown on Page 65)

(7) Digital calipers

(8) Pair of compasses (especially for the later shoji and kumiko patterns)

(9) 2B pencil

Photograph 37 Layout tools

Gennō (hammers)

(1) Approx. 150 gm. *gennō* — For adjusting the *kanna* blade and tapping in kumiko

(2) 185–250 gm. *gennō* or hammer

(3) Hardwood block (150 x 60 x 40 mm)

Photograph 38 *Gennō* and *kanna*

Kanna (or Western equivalent)

(1) 70 mm *hira-ganna* (or your preferred size)

(2) *Dainaoshi kanna* (if using *kanna*; not needed if using Western planes)

(3) *Kiwa-ganna* — left and right (or shoulder plane)

(4) * *Kakumen-ganna* (chamfer plane) — I recommend the Japanese version because of its high degree of accuracy

(5) Approx. 42 mm small *kanna* (*ko-ganna*) and/or block plane

Nokogiri (saws)

(1) * Fine-tooth cross-cut *dōzuki* saw — This saw will be used for cutting the joints in kumiko, and I recommend the Japanese version because it gives a much finer cut (I use the Nakaya Eaks Kumiko saw D-210C 210 mm, and it is an excellent saw)

(2) 240 mm cross-cut *dōzuki* saw (or the Western equivalent)

(3) 210 mm rip-cut *dōzuki* saw (or the Western equivalent)

(4) *Ryōba* (if preferred)

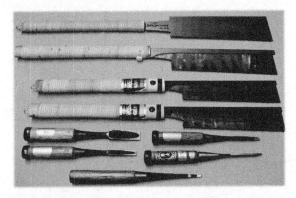

Photograph 39 *Nokogiri* and chisels

Chisels (Japanese or Western)

(1) *Ōire nomi* (butt chisels) — 3 mm, 6 mm, 9 mm, 19 mm

(2) *Sokosarai nomi* — This chisel is used for cleaning up the bottom of mortises; handy to have, but not essential

Miscellaneous

(1) Shoji paper

(2) Shoji glue (any starch glue will suffice)

(3) Sharpening stones

(4) Small clamps (*hatagane*) — For securing kumiko to the kumiko jig.

(5) Cutters — For cutting shoji paper

(6) Brush — For applying shoji glue to kumiko

(7) Metal straightedge (or wide paint scraper) — For use in trimming shoji paper after applying to the kumiko

(8) Water atomizer

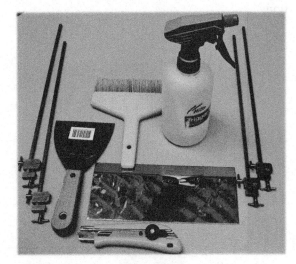

Photograph 40 Miscellaneous tools

Jigs

Kumiko cutting jig

This is your main jig, and you will use it every time you cut the tenons and half-lap housing joints in kumiko. You can use either MDF or very stable hardwood for this jig.

The ends of the kumiko butt up against the end stop, so make sure it is secured to the base piece at exactly 90° to the side support, and that the face is exactly 90° to the base. The side support (16 x 22 mm) is secured to the side of the base by glue and screws. The face of the end stop is chamfered at the bottom to prevent sawdust accumulation.

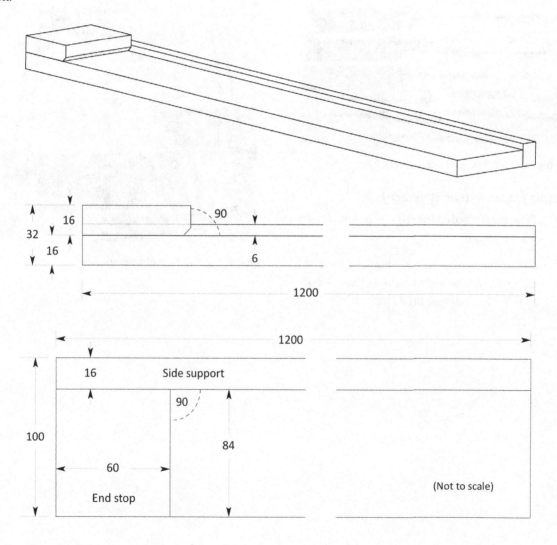

Diagram 54 Kumiko cutting jig

Jaguchi rail jig

This jig is for cutting the 45° angles in the ends of the rails. For ease of use, two jigs are required: the wider (75 mm) is for the bottom rails, and the narrower (50 mm) for the top rails and any center rails if included. Depending on the width of your saw, you may need to make the base thinner, say, 25 mm instead of 30 mm.

The bottom of the jig rests on the top of the rail so the 45° angle must be set from the bottom surface as shown in the diagram. The side support holds the jig against the side of the rail. It can be 6–10 mm thick, whichever you find most comfortable. I prefer the side support to sit just above the top of the base, but this can be trimmed flush if you prefer.

This jig can be made from any stable timber — hardwood or softwood.

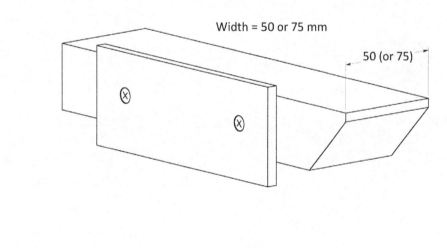

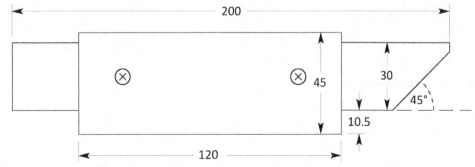

Diagram 55 *Jaguchi* rail jig

Chamfering jig

The chamfering jig supports the pieces when chamfering. The dimensions in the diagram below are meant as a guide only. The actual size or depth of the jig required will depend on the size of the pieces you use in your shoji. I have several jigs of varying depths to give stable support for the wider rails, and also for the narrow kumiko.

The end rests against a stop on the workbench, and the piece being chamfered rests up against the end stop on the jig.

I make my chamfering jigs on the table-saw with the blade set at 45°, and I use a piece of the offcut for the end stop. When setting the table-saw blade at an angle, there is always the potential for kick-back, so take extreme care when making the cuts for this jig. The top edge can become quite sharp, so chamfer the tops as shown to prevent any injury.

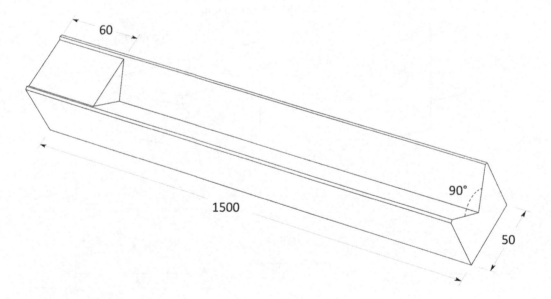

Diagram 56 Chamfering jig

Tsukeko mitering jig

The *tsukeko* mitering jig is for cutting the miters on the *tsukeko* where a mortise and tenon is required. The jig itself is very simple, and should take no more than a couple of minutes to make. You should make sure that the angle is exactly 45°, as the accuracy of this angle will have a direct influence on the quality of the miter joint. The jig has been designed so that you can clamp the *tsukeko* to the jig with a small *hatagane* to hold it secure as you cut the miter tenons and mortises.

The rebate into which the *tsukeko* fits should be slightly shallower than the thickness (*mitsuke*) of the *tsukeko* so that the jig can be held firmly on top of it. In this case the *tsukeko mitsuke* is 6.4 mm, so make the rebate 6 mm deep.

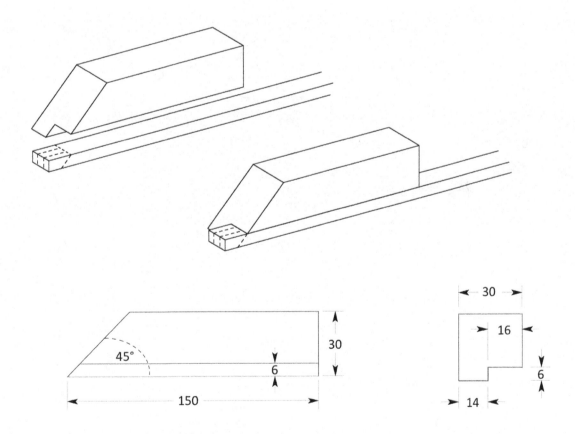

Diagram 57 *Tsukeko* mitering jig

45° shooting board

I use these jigs to trim the ends of *tsukeko* where a mortise and tenon is not required. There are countless shooting board designs on the internet, ranging from very simple to highly complex. These are diagrams of the two I use; very simple, but they work.

I use a Western style block plane with the first jig, so I've attached a bench stop on the bottom to stabilize it when planing. It is very straightforward as shown in the diagram. I've cut a 6 x 6 mm groove in the base where the plane runs so that end-grain shavings won't interfere with the process. The second jig is used with a *kanna*, and is even simpler than the first jig. Two different ways of approaching the same task.

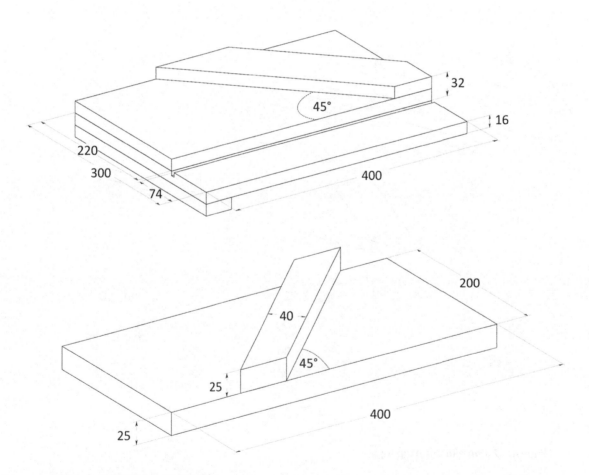

Diagram 58 45° shooting board

Marking gauge jig

This is a handy and adjustable jig for marking the mortise and tenon locations on the rails and stiles. The dimensions in the diagram are merely a guide, so make any refinements you feel are necessary.

Make an opening for the marking rod in roughly the center of the base fence, then insert, and adjust the marking rod as necessary. The fit must be very tight so there is no movement. Adjust the marking rod inward or outward by tapping it on your workbench or other solid object as appropriate.

The marking pins are simply small nails hammered into the marking rod and cut off with pliers or other form of cutter to form a pointed edge. In the diagram, the four marking pins have been set at the correct intervals for the rail and stile mortises and tenons in the shoji we make in this book. You can make minor adjustments to these intervals by using the pliers to bend the nails slightly as required.

For better and more accurate results when using the jig, rotate the jig slightly so the marking pins are at an angle rather than perpendicular to the piece being marked.

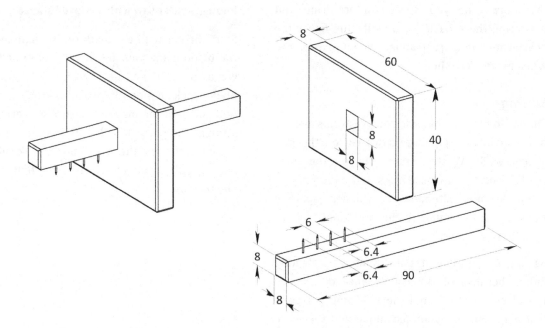

Diagram 59 Marking gauge jig

Exercises

As I mentioned in the Introduction, without access to the highly expensive purpose-built machinery available in Japan, we have to rely heavily on hand tools and our hand skills when making shoji. This is no different from what *tateguya* and kumiko *shokunin* had to do in past centuries, and their work was extremely tight and perfectly crafted, and has stood the test of time. So while making shoji by hand may be more time-consuming, with the right skills and practice, it is certainly not beyond anyone's reach to make the kind of shoji you can fit with pride anywhere in your home.

The following are a few exercises that we had to repeat regularly at the college in Japan where I studied shoji (Shokugei Gakuin). I still go through these exercises on a regular basis to make sure the hand skills I've developed don't decline, especially considering the precision and concentration required in the more intricate patterns I include in my artwork, which all have to be done by hand.

I encourage you to complete these exercises several times before starting the shoji because the more time you spend on acquiring and mastering these basic hand skills, the fewer the heartaches and frustrations you'll experience when making the shoji.

Sawing

Similar to planes, Japanese and Western saws are different in that Japanese saws cut on the pull stroke while Western saws cut on the push stroke. I prefer Japanese saws, but either can be used for shoji, although the thinner Japanese saws are more suited to the fine kumiko work than Western saws.

Sawing is a skill that unfortunately is steadily fading because of the convenience of modern power cutting tools, but the following exercises will help improve your technique and therefore your kumiko and rail joinery. For the first few exercises, use a piece of softwood about 60 mm wide, about 30 mm thick, and any reasonable length.

For shoji work with Japanese saws, your stance when sawing should be relaxed, and you should hold the saw with the same pressure you would use when holding an egg; firm, but not so tight that the egg would break. The saw handle should sit comfortably in your hand and your forefinger should extend along the top or along the side, whichever feels more natural. When cutting, you should hold your arms lightly into your sides, and from the front, the saw, your hand and your elbow should form a straight line.

Photograph 41 Saw with a relaxed stance

Start the cut with the teeth on the handle end of the blade using your left-hand thumb or forefinger as a guide, and use the entire length of the blade in clean smooth strokes, closely observing both sides of the blade to ensure you are cutting straight and perpendicular. At no time should you force the cut, and the return push stroke after the cutting pull stroke should be very light without any tension.

Photograph 42 Saw, hand and elbow form a straight line

Cutting on and to a line

The first exercise is simply cutting on and to a line. With the marking gauge, mark a line along both sides of the practice piece about 7.5 mm down from the face. Make five marks across the face at about 5 mm intervals using the marking knife and try square. With your kumiko saw, cut along the face line down to the lines on the sides.

Check to make sure the depth of cut is equal on both sides, and that the cut is exactly perpendicular to the face on both sides. Cut all five marks, then make five more marks and repeat.

This exercise will help you with the kumiko cuts, and the cuts on one side of the rail tenons. I made thousands of these practice cuts at the College, and I still do this exercise regularly.

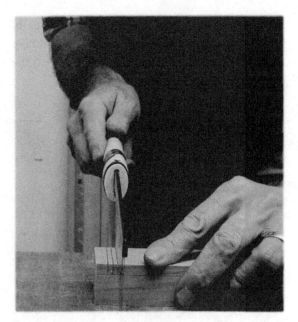

Photograph 43 Cutting on and to a line

Cutting kumiko half-lap joints

The second exercise is cutting out the half-lap housing joints for kumiko. For this exercise use a piece of wood with the same dimensions as in the previous exercise, but you will also need to prepare a kumiko. The kumiko *mitsuke* (see Diagram 50 on Page 52) is 6.4 mm, *mikomi* 15 mm, and the piece should be about 400 mm long.

Mark along both sides of the practice piece 7.5 mm down from the face. Make five marks across the face at 25 mm intervals, and cut along all face lines down to the 7.5 mm line, checking to make sure that the depth of cut is equal on both sides. This is the left-hand side of the kumiko joint.

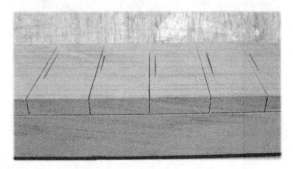

Photograph 44 Cut on left-hand side

Flip the piece around, place the left-hand side of the kumiko against the square and gradually move it over until the right-hand side of the kumiko just hides the cut.

Photograph 45 Use kumiko to gauge width of joint

This is the critical part in cutting kumiko joints. If you move it over too far, the joint will be too tight, and the kumiko will bend up or snap, and if it's not over far enough, you will have unsightly gaps in your kumiko joinery.

Once it's properly lined up, hold the square firmly in place, remove the kumiko, and mark along the square. This is the right-hand side of the kumiko joint.

Photograph 46 Mark right-hand side

Cut along this mark to the required 7.5 mm depth, then remove the waste with a 6 mm chisel.

Photograph 47 Cut right-hand side

Repeat this for all five cuts.

Photograph 48 Remove the waste

Test each of the joints with the kumiko. The kumiko should fit firmly without the need for force.

Photograph 49 Fit should be firm but not too tight

This exercise will give you further practice in using the saw, and it will also give you the judgment required for making clean and tight kumiko joints.

Cutting the jaguchi

The next exercise is cutting at 45° to the face. This cut is necessary for the small extension — called a *jaguchi* (also called an *umanori* chamfer) — on the front face of the rails, and you will need the *jaguchi* rail jig. In Japan there is a machine that cuts these *jaguchi* joints and the tenons with a single pass, but it's not readily available in the West, and its high cost puts it out of reach of anyone but the fully established *tateguya*.

Mark the sides of the practice piece 3 mm down from the face. Make five marks across the face at about 5 mm intervals using the marking knife and try square. With the 240 mm *dōzuki* saw make one or two light cuts along the face mark to establish the kerf.

Photograph 50 Establish the kerf

Now turn the saw so that it is at 45° to the face, and make two or three light cuts to establish the 45° cut.

Photograph 51 Establish the 45° cut

Without removing the saw, move the *jaguchi* jig up to the saw so that the blade sits flush against the jig's 45° edge. Holding the jig firmly, complete the cut down to the 3 mm mark, making sure that the depth of cut is equal on both sides. Repeat for all five marks, then make five more marks and repeat.

Photograph 52 Use the jig to complete the 45° cut

Rip sawing

The final sawing exercise is rip sawing with the rip-cut saw. Square the end of the practice piece and mark 21 mm from the end on all faces, ensuring that the marks are square. With the marking gauge, mark the ends and along the side down to the 21 mm line with four marks. Although not particularly important, for consistency make these marks the same widths as the shoji rail double tenons: from the front face, 6 mm, 6.4 mm, 6 mm, and 6.4 mm.

Photograph 53 Mark tenon cheeks

Cut along these lines down to the 21 mm line. Rip-cut sawing is much more difficult to control than cross-cut sawing so work slowly and carefully.

I've found an easy way to make the rip cut in tenons is to secure the piece so it overhangs the bench, and cut along the line pulling in a down-ward motion. This way the pulling forces of the saw are acting against the solid workbench top, so the piece will remain stable throughout the cut.

Photograph 54 Cut down to 21 mm shoulder line

Once you have made all the cuts to the 21 mm line, cut the end off and repeat.

Mortises and tenons

Almost all of the shoji frames I describe in this book use double tenons to connect the rails and stiles, and firm tight-fitting joints are essential. This exercise is simply cutting double tenons by hand and fitting them into mortises also made by hand. The mortise and tenon dimensions are standard mortise and tenon dimensions for shoji in the Kanto region of Tokyo and surrounding prefectures, as are all the dimensions I use in this book, so the practice here will be of direct use in the shoji.

Standard joint

The first exercise is a standard mortise and tenon joint. The mortise piece has the stile dimensions of 30.5 x 30.5 mm, and the tenon piece is the top rail with dimensions of 45 x 29 mm. The tenon

dimensions are shown in the diagram. Mark the face of the practice stile as shown in the diagram, and cut the mortises with a chisel to a depth of 22 mm, ensuring that the ends and sides are clean and perpendicular to the face.

Square the end of the practice rail, and mark and cut the tenons to the dimensions shown in the diagram.

Take care when cleaning the waste between the tenons that you don't cut past the mark or damage the edge. When the tenons have been cut, lightly chamfer the ends on all sides and test fit. The rail piece should fit firmly and flush against the face and flush with the front side, without being too tight so that it has to be forced in, or too loose so that it can be easily jiggled.

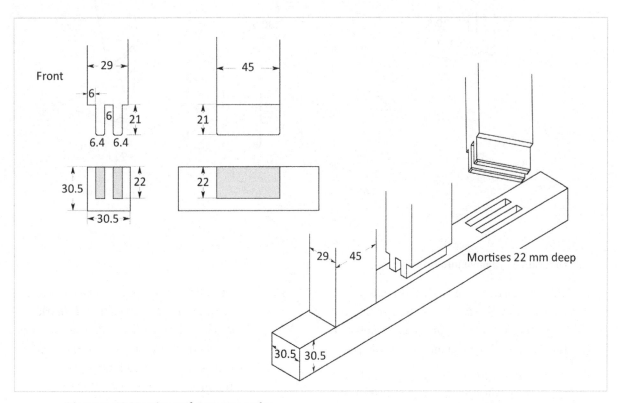

Diagram 60 Mortise and tenon exercise

71

Jaguchi joint

The aim of this exercise is to practice making the mortises and tenons exactly as they are made in the shoji in this book (except the haunch). This is almost the same as the previous exercise, except instead of a standard joint, we make a *jaguchi* joint on the rail and a corresponding chamfer on the stile to fit the *jaguchi*. I'll list this procedure in steps because it must be done in a specific sequence.

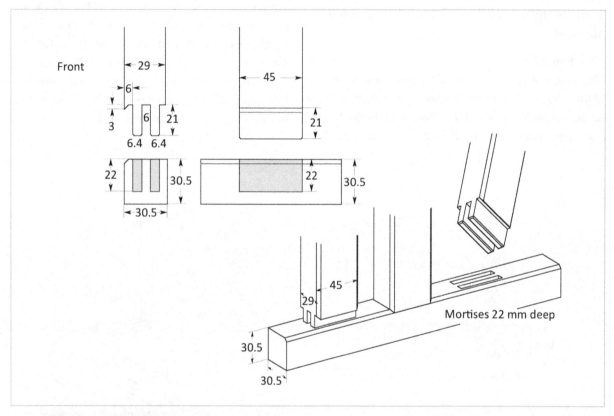

Diagram 61 *Jaguchi* joint exercise

(1) Cut the mortises in exactly the same way as was done in the standard joint exercise and according to the measurements shown in the diagram. Do not chamfer the stile yet.

(2) Square the end of the practice rail, and mark the tenon shoulders 21 mm from the end on the back face and the two sides. DO NOT mark the front face.

(3) On one of the sides, place a mark exactly 3 mm from the tenon shoulder mark toward the rail end. In effect, this mark is 18 mm from the end, but for the *jaguchi* mark it is always better to measure from the tenon shoulder mark rather than the end.

72

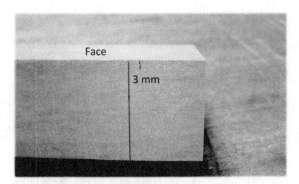

Photograph 55 Mark the tenon shoulders on the sides and back

(4)   Extend this mark across the front face. This is the *jaguchi* mark.

Photograph 56 Mark the 3mm *jaguchi* extension

(5)   Mark the tenon cheeks on the end and two sides according to the dimensions in the diagram. Because the back of the rail is off-set 1.5 mm from the back of the stile, make sure you work from the front face.

(6)   Cut the *jaguchi* as was done in the *jaguchi* exercise. Take care with this, because the quality of the cut here will show clearly in the quality of the join with the corresponding chamfer.

Photograph 57 Cut the *jaguchi* mark at 45°

(7)   Cut the tenon shoulder down to the tenon cheek on the back face.

(8)   Cut the tenons as in the previous exercise.

(9)   Remove the waste between the tenons with a 6 mm chisel. A bandsaw can be used both to cut the tenons and remove the waste, but because the aim of these exercises is to improve hand skills, I recommend doing this by hand, and save the use of routers, bandsaws and other power tools for actually making the shoji.

(10)   If the *jaguchi* and tenon markings were accurate, there should be a 3 mm space between the *jaguchi* and the tenon, so clean the waste out with a 3 mm chisel, taking care not to damage the *jaguchi*.

(11)   Lightly chamfer the ends of the tenons on all sides

Photograph 58 Tenons with *jaguchi*

(12) Chamfer the rail piece on the front face and two sides with the *kakumen-ganna*. You do not need to chamfer the back (in actual shoji the backs are lightly chamfered, but not with this plane). This is a gradual process of adjusting the plane in small increments.

Photograph 60 Extent of chamfer

(14) Without adjusting the plane, chamfer the front of the stile piece. If you don't chamfer the stile enough, the *jaguchi* extension will split, but if you chamfer too much, there will be a gap between the *jaguchi* and the stile chamfer. The difference between too much and not enough here is no more than the thickness of one or two plane shavings, so work slowly and carefully.

(15) Test fit the two pieces. If all measuring and cutting has been accurate, the two pieces will fit together cleanly and the join between the chamfer and *jaguchi* will be snug and gap-free.

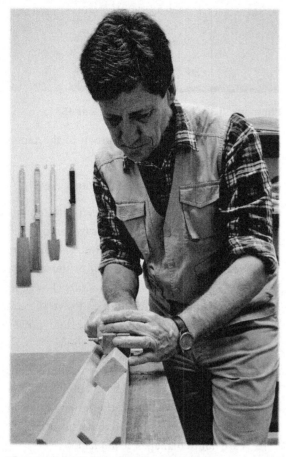

Photograph 59 Chamfer edges

(13) Chamfer down until the edge of the chamfer is in line with the corner where the *jaguchi* meets the tenon shoulder as shown in the following photograph.

Photograph 61 Work carefully to avoid damage to the *jaguchi*

Photograph 62 A firm fit

This is a critical process, and it takes a great deal of practice to consistently achieve a tight joint, so I urge you to repeat this exercise several times before making a shoji with this joint. It gives clean lines to a rail and stile construction, so its application goes beyond shoji, and it can add considerable interest to a cabinet or the like with frame and panel joinery. Router bits are available that give the same or a similar cut, but I firmly believe the sense of accomplishment gained from being able to cut this joint by hand is certainly worth the time needed to become proficient in making it.

Calculating dimensions

When making shoji to fit traditional grooves the important dimensions are those of the actual opening, be it a door or window. To calculate the height of the shoji, measure the height of the opening and add 11 mm (see Diagram 62: Height of opening + 8 mm + 3 mm). This accounts for the top and bottom grooves and the depths that the rebates are seated. If the threshold and head jamb are not parallel, and one side of the head jamb is slightly higher than the other, calculate for the higher side and trim to fit at the end. The need for adjustment, especially in Japan where house movement can be quite substantial because of the frequent earthquakes, is why shoji stiles always have 10 mm horns on the top and 5 mm horns on the bottom. For the various mechanical tracking systems, you will need to read the instructions for the system you are using and make the necessary calculations.

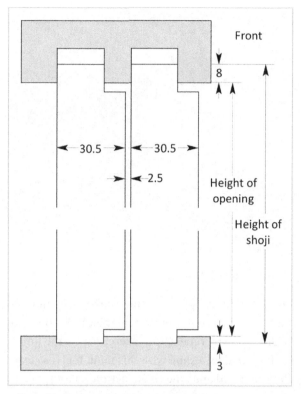

Diagram 62 Height of shoji

To calculate the width of each shoji in a set, measure the width of the opening, add the total width of the overlapping stiles, and divide by the number of screens.

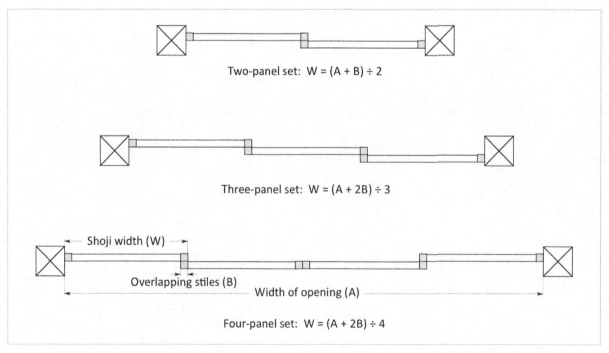

Two-panel set: W = (A + B) ÷ 2

Three-panel set: W = (A + 2B) ÷ 3

Four-panel set: W = (A + 2B) ÷ 4

Diagram 63 Width of shoji

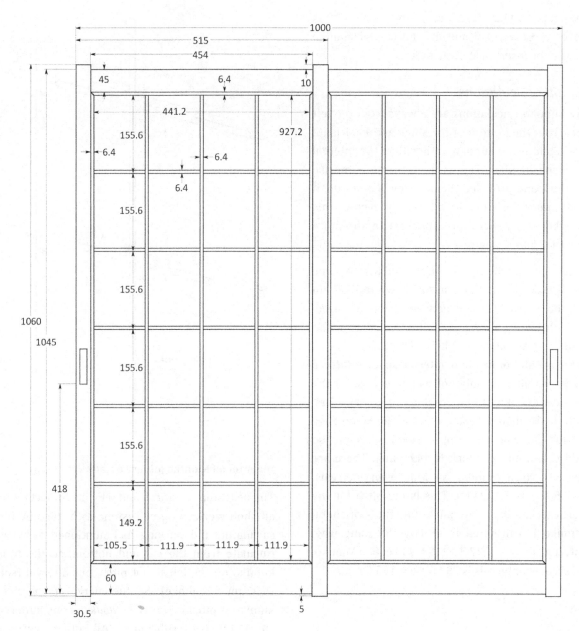

Diagram 64 Shoji dimension details

Overall shoji size

The opening for this pair of shoji is a width of 1000 mm and a height of 1034 mm. As shown in Diagram 63, for two shoji, W = (A + B) ÷ 2, therefore W = (1000 + 30.5) ÷ 2, which is 515.25 mm. We can safely ignore the .25 mm, so the width of each shoji is 515 mm. The height is simply 1034 + 11, which is 1045 mm. Each shoji therefore has to be 1045 x 515 mm (the horns are not included in this calculation).

Once the overall size of the shoji has been determined, we need to work out the internal dimensions, and from this, the kumiko intervals. The internal width is the width of the shoji (515 mm) minus the widths of the two stiles and two *tsukeko* (61+12.8 mm), so the calculation is 515 - 73.8 = 441.2 mm. The internal height is the height of the shoji (1045 mm) minus the widths of the upper and lowers rails (45 + 60 mm) and the two *tsukeko* (12.8 mm), so the calculation is 1045 - 117.8 = 927.2 mm. The internal space is therefore 441.2 x 927.2 mm, and within this space three vertical and five horizontal kumiko have to be inserted at even intervals.

Kumiko calculations

My kumiko calculations are always from the left and from the bottom of the shoji, and I calculate the pitch of the kumiko, rather than the interval between kumiko. This is a much more precise method, and provided the marking is accurate, it guarantees the kumiko will line up evenly. This will become much more apparent in the more complex kumiko patterns.

Calculating pitch is quite simple, and it's the same for both width and height. As shown in Diagram 64, the internal space is between the two *tsukeko* on either side, not between the two stiles or the two rails, so be careful here. The calculation is: pitch = width or height of internal space + *mitsuke* of one kumiko ÷ number of even intervals. For the vertical kumiko, the internal space is 441.2 mm, and the kumiko *mitsuke* (see Diagram 50 on Page 52 for the explanation of *mitsuke*) is 6.4 mm, so add 6.4 to 441.2, which is 447.6 mm. There are three vertical kumiko, so four even intervals: 447.6 ÷ 4 is 111.9 mm. This is the pitch for the vertical kumiko. The pitch for the horizontal kumiko is calculated in exactly the same way: internal space of 927.2 + 6.4 = 933.6, five kumiko, so six even intervals is 933.6 ÷ 6 = 155.6 mm.

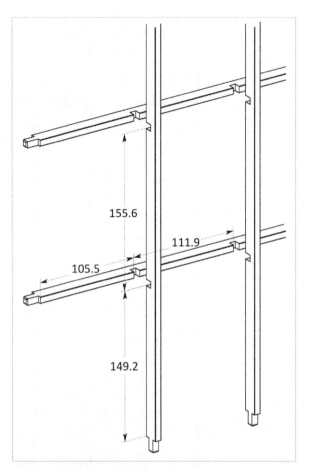

Diagram 65 Kumiko joinery details

The next step is critical, and why it's important in all shoji work to be consistent with the side for calculating and marking. As I mentioned, I always calculate from the left and bottom, so the first kumiko on the left is not pitch, but interval (see Diagram 65 above). So the mark for the first kumiko is pitch minus the *mitsuke* of one kumiko, so 111.9 - 6.4 = 105.5 mm. All other vertical kumiko are marked with the pitch. The same applies to the horizontal kumiko. The mark for the first kumiko from the bottom is 155.6 - 6.4 = 149.2 mm. All other horizontal kumiko are marked with the pitch.

Calculating dimensions

This section on calculating dimensions may appear at times to be "stating the obvious", but there is a reason for going into this much detail. As in all woodworking endeavors, in making shoji, accuracy in marking is the key to success. But with shoji, the large number of interlocking joints in the kumiko lattice makes this accuracy doubly important. A small inaccuracy in kumiko joinery will be noticeable by a kink in otherwise straight kumiko at best, and at worst, the confidence-destroying sound of snapping wood. This first shoji has only eight kumiko at wide intervals, so the calculations are simple, but in the shoji I explain later in the book the number of kumiko steadily increases, and in some of the highly complex patterns, the base kumiko can number over one hundred.

Using pitch instead of interval when marking kumiko makes this process much easier. If we were to mark using interval, we would also have to mark both sides of each kumiko instead of just the one side. This virtually doubles the amount of measuring and marking we have to do, and therefore doubles the possibility of error.

Why 30.5 mm and not 30.0 mm for stiles?

This was the measurement we used at Shokugei Gakuin for shoji stiles. Most shoji design books, however, use 30 mm for stiles. Why the difference?

In fact, there is no difference, because *tateguya* use neither 30.5 mm nor 30.0 mm. Along with carpenters and some more senior furniture makers, *tateguya* still use Japan's old form of measurement of *shaku*, *sun*, *bu*, and *rin*. In the Kanto region the thickness of a standard stile in a full-sized shoji is 1 *sun*, or 30.3022 mm, and being the stickler for accuracy that he is, Sawada Sensei, my instructor at the College, required us to use 30.5 mm instead of 30.0 mm if we were using the metric measurement system. This also allowed us a small amount to shave off with a plane for final adjustment if necessary. The 29 mm width of rails is actually 9 *bu* 5 *rin* or 9.5 *bu*, which is 28.78709 mm, so we use 29 mm.

Preparing the timber

Milling

Different timbers are available in different regions, so it would be of little value in trying to list every type of timber and its suitability, and beyond the scope of this book and certainly beyond the scope of my knowledge and experience. Regardless of the timber available to you, it should be stable, properly seasoned, and have a straight and tight grain without blemishes. Softwoods are certainly easier to work with, but hardwoods can also be used, and can be very effective. Traditionally, shoji are hand-plane finished with no sanding or varnish, so if you intend to finish with a hand-plane, you must select a timber that planes well; if you intend to use a finish, you have more options available to you.

The grain on the fronts of the stiles should be straight and clean, as should the fronts of the rails, so plan your cuts to achieve this. If unavoidable, a small amount of grain pattern on the front of the rails is acceptable, but it should be very subtle.

The cut for the kumiko is another one of those decisions based on regional differences and preferences. For normal kumiko patterns I prefer the *mitsuke* to have the straight grain, and I plan my cuts accordingly. On the detailed, intricate kumiko work I prefer it the other way around; the straight grain on the *mikomi*, as it leaves a better and cleaner cut with the special planes I use. Either way is acceptable though.

When milling the timber on the machinery, I leave the face and sides slightly oversize by about 0.2 mm, and this extra is taken off when I do the final planing before assembly. I also leave an extra 50 mm or so on the ends of the various pieces for ease of working. So the minimum timber required for the rails and stiles is as follows.

Cutting List (in millimeters)

Component	L	W	T	N
Top rail	550	45	29	2
Bottom rail	550	60	29	2
Stile	1,110	30.5	30.5	4
Vertical kumiko	1,100	6.4	15	6
Horizontal kumiko	550	6.4	14	10
Tsukeko	1,100	6.4	16	6
Story stick	1,300	20	20	1

L: Length (cut oversize); W: Width (*mitsuke*); T: Thickness (*mikomi*); N: Number (this is the minimum number required)

Table 2 *Mizugoshi* shoji cutting list

The kumiko *mitsuke* dimension is absolutely critical, and must be exact. I have a small benchtop surface planer, and a *hikōki kanna* (a plane with a spring on the sole to hold the kumiko stable and adjustable fences on the sides to adjust thickness — see Photograph 4 on Page 8), but I find I use my drum sander the most.

Marking

Examine the rail, stiles and *tsukeko*, and decide on the fronts, backs and orientation of all pieces, and mark in your preferred way. Also mark which parts will go with the first and second shoji. *Tateguya* have a system of a single mark on the rear face and a joining double mark on the inner side, but I have always used the triangle mark and I find it a much easier marking system. Use the marks that you find easiest to understand.

Story stick

Mark the story stick with all stile, rail and kumiko markings with a sharp marking knife in accordance with Diagram 64 — one side for all vertical dimensions, another side for all horizontal dimensions.

Remember to mark from the left for the horizontal dimensions and from the bottom for the vertical dimensions, as shown in the examples in the following diagram. To avoid confusion, place a pencil mark on the side of the mark that the kumiko sits.

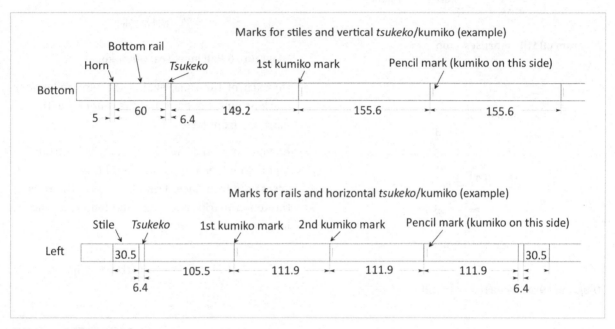

Diagram 66 Story stick

Stiles

All marks should be made on the inner side of the rails and stiles. Clamp the story stick to one of the stiles and transfer the markings to the stile. Use this stile to mark the other three stiles, making sure that the top and bottom orientation is correct.

Mark the mortise locations on all stiles as shown in the following diagrams. Diagram 68 does not show the dimensions for the mortise thickness and position at the stile top, but they are the same as those shown for the stile bottom in Diagram 67.

Trim the ends of the stiles at the horn marks, and chamfer around the top and bottom edges.

Note that the backs of the horizontal kumiko are 3 mm from the back of the stile, so the kumiko mortises are positioned 7.3 mm from the back of the stile. You will need to be very accurate with this, otherwise you will have difficulties when assembling the shoji. You will also need to be very accurate with the location of the mortise for the *tsukeko*.

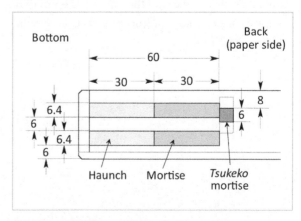

Diagram 67 Stile mortises – bottom

81

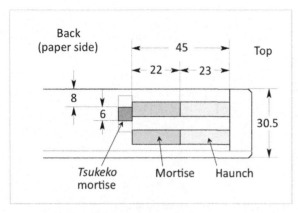

Diagram 68 Stile mortises – top

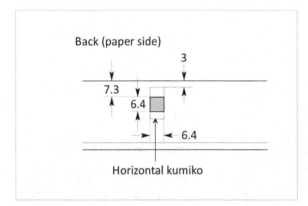

Diagram 69 Stile mortises – kumiko

Rails

Clamp the story stick to one of the rails and transfer the tenon and mortise markings to the rail as was done for the stiles in the previous step, then use this rail to mark the other rails, ensuring you have the correct left and right orientation.

Note that the backs of the vertical kumiko are 1.5 mm from the back of the rail, so the kumiko mortises are cut 5.8 mm from the back, as shown in Diagram 70.

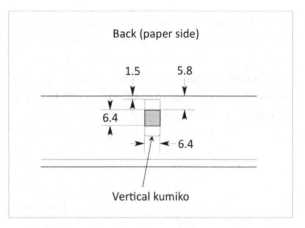

Diagram 70 Rail mortises – kumiko

On each of the rails, extend the tenon shoulder mark around the back and the outer side. Do not mark the front face.

As you did in the exercises, mark 3 mm from the tenon shoulder marks for the *jaguchi*, and mark across the front face. Trim the ends of the rails to the tenon marks, and mark the tenons as shown in Diagram 71.

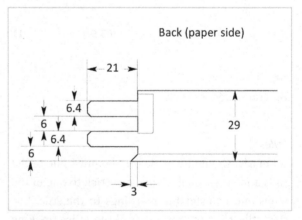

Diagram 71 Rail tenons

Tsukeko

Clamp the story stick to the appropriate *tsukeko* and transfer the markings as was done in the previous steps for the rails and stiles. Make sure you have the correct left/right and top/bottom orientation for each. The backs of the kumiko are flush with the backs of the *tsukeko*, so the mortises are cut 4.3 mm from the back edge, as shown in Diagrams 72 and 73.

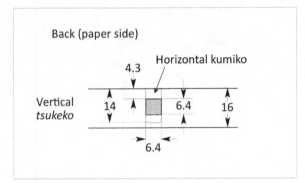

Diagram 72 Vertical *tsukeko* mortises

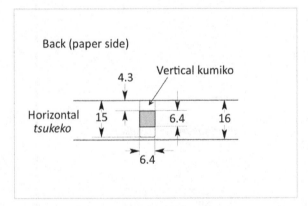

Diagram 73 Horizontal *tsukeko* mortises

Mark the *tsukeko* end miters to the dimensions shown in the following diagram. The cutting process is shown from Page 86.

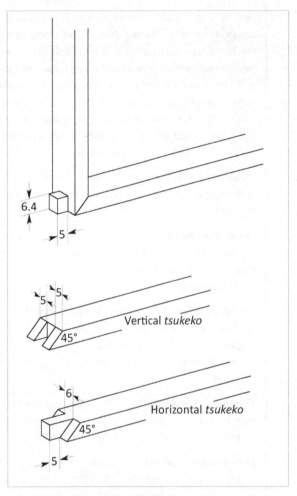

Diagram 74 *Tsukeko* miter joint

To include *tsukeko* or not?

This is a personal preference that is influenced by design considerations and the overall atmosphere of the room where the shoji will be fitted. Personally, I believe that *tsukeko* give a heightened feeling of quality and style, so I fit them to all my shoji. The *tsukeko mitsuke* is normally the same as the kumiko, or slightly smaller if the kumiko *mitsuke* is quite wide, although this is not a hard and fast rule and if the design calls for it, any size within reason is acceptable.

There are several methods of attaching *tsukeko* to the main frame; the diagrams on the right show the kinds of *tsukeko* most widely used.

The **tsuba-tsukeko** is the one I use in this book, and is the most commonly used and least time-consuming type. Without care, though, gaps can open up between the *tsukeko* and the rails or styles.

The **ōire-tsukeko** (also called the *hon-tsukeko*) fits in a shallow groove made in the stiles and reduces the risk of gaps, but the edge of the groove is quite weak and can easily break off if the fit is too tight or the groove is too deep.

The **shakuridashi-tsukeko** is formed from the rail and stile by rebates, and is considered to be one of the better methods, but it is very time-consuming.

The **kamihari-jakuri** is actually no *tsukeko*. The kumiko tenons are mortised directly into the rails and stiles. A shallow rebate is made in the stiles in line with the backs of the rails and kumiko, and the edge of the shoji paper is glued to the rails and to this rebate. This is the simplest and least time-consuming method of attaching the kumiko lattice to the main frame.

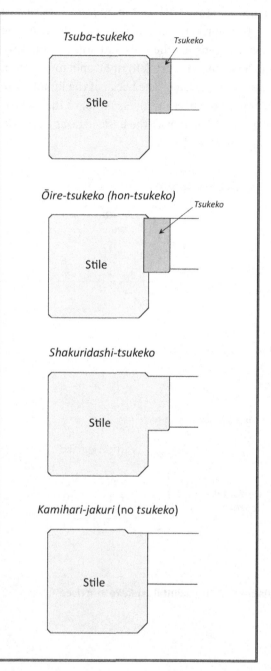

Tsuba-tsukeko

Ōire-tsukeko (hon-tsukeko)

Shakuridashi-tsukeko

Kamihari-jakuri (no *tsukeko*)

Cutting the frames

Mortises and tenons

Stiles

Cut out the mortises for the rail tenons, *tsukeko* and kumiko in the stiles using your preferred method. The mortises for the rail tenons are 22 mm deep, and the haunch housing is a fraction deeper than 8 mm. The mortises for the *tsukeko* are 5.5 mm deep. The mortises for the kumiko are 7.5 mm deep. There is a 1.5 mm offset between the backs of the stiles and the rails, and also between the backs of the rails and *tsukeko*, so take extra care with the position of the mortises in relation to the back.

Rails

Cut the mortises for the kumiko to a depth of 7.5 mm.

Cut the *jaguchi* on the rails as explained in the exercise from Page 72, then cut the tenons and trim the haunches to the dimensions shown in the following diagram. Take care not to damage the *jaguchi* extension when you work on the tenons, especially when trimming the haunches. Also make sure that the haunches are cut on the correct edges, i.e. the outside edges.

Photograph 63 Cut the haunches

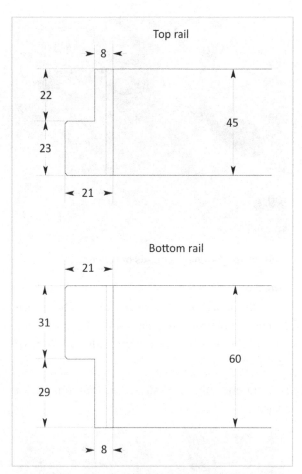

Diagram 75 Rail tenon dimensions

The measurement for the tenons in the diagram is not a typing error; the tenons are each 1 mm wider than the mating mortises. This extra 1 mm is compressed as the rail is inserted in the stile, and pushes the inner side up against the inner edge of the mortise giving a very clean and flush joint. In this way, clamping is unnecessary; the fit holds the frame together firmly until the glue dries. You do, however, have to make sure that your marking and cutting is very precise, because there is no test fit, otherwise the whole purpose of slightly oversizing the tenon width is defeated. For hardwood, this extra width can be reduced to 0.5 mm. DO NOT oversize the thickness of the tenons.

Chamfer the ends of the tenons, but do not chamfer the sides of the stiles and rails — these are chamfered at the end just before assembly.

Photograph 64 Chamfer ends of tenons

Tsukeko

Cut the mortises in the *tsukeko*. These are through mortises, so make sure the back face where the mortise came through is clean of waste.

Cut the end miters as shown in Diagram 74 on Page 83.

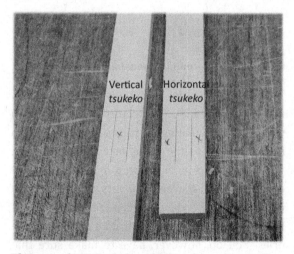

Photograph 65 *Tsukeko* miter marks

Pencil in a 45° line on the sides from the end mark on all *tsukeko*. This doesn't need to be an exact mark, but make sure it is on the waste side.

Photograph 66 Pencil in the 45° line

The horizontal *tsukeko* is the more complex of the two. Cut along the pencil line on both sides down to the tenon mark.

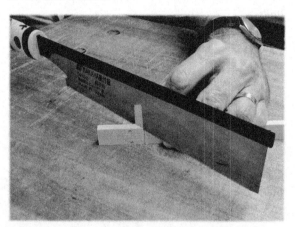

Photograph 67 Cut down to the tenon marks

Mark the 5 mm tenon extension on the back, and cut.

Photograph 68 Mark the tenon extension

Cut along the tenon lines (Photograph 69), then use the *tsukeko* mitering jig and a sharp chisel to pare to the line (Photograph 70).

Photograph 69 Cut along the tenon cheek lines

Photograph 70 Pare to the line with the jig

The cuts for the vertical *tsukeko* are much simpler. First, cut off the ends at 45° along the pencil line.

Photograph 71 Cut the ends at 45° for the vertical *tsukeko*

Next, trim to the line using either the *tsukeko* mitering jig or the 45° shooting board.

Photograph 72 Trim the ends on the shooting board

Cut along the tenon lines, then remove the center waste with a sharp chisel, ensuring that the cut is 90° to the face.

Photograph 73 Remove center waste

This miter joint for the *tsukeko* is time-consuming, but because the *aragumi* pattern has such wide intervals between kumiko, the corners can be quite weak where they are attached to the rails and stiles, so cutting the joint this way and inserting the tenon parts into mortises in the stiles prevents the corners from becoming detached. This becomes less necessary with the other patterns where the kumiko interval is much smaller, and tapping in thin tacks or nails into the *tsukeko* miters is a quick and acceptable method.

Rebates

Cut the rebates in the rails as shown in Photograph 74 and Diagram 76. These fit into the grooves in the head jamb and threshold. Make sure you cut them on the front side of the rails. The rebates are normally cut in the stiles on-site to allow for adjustment, so sawing and planing techniques are critical. The rebate cut leaves a tongue of 19.5 mm on the rails, which extends to 21 mm on the stiles, considering the 1.5 mm offset between the back of the rail and stile. This leaves a very tight fit, but the rebates are trimmed on-site as necessary when adjusting the shoji.

Photograph 74 Rebates in rails

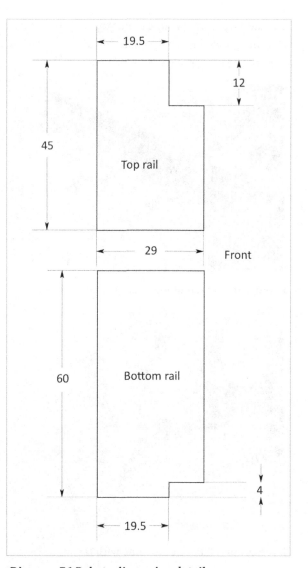

Diagram 76 Rebate dimension details

Raising the grain

Place the *tsukeko* safely to one side. Thoroughly wet a piece of cloth and wipe the water liberally over the rails and stiles, then place to one side and allow to dry. The reason for this is to raise the grain so that the final planing will leave a highly polished surface, and also to remove all of the machining marks.

This completes work on the frames until the pre-assembly step, and it's now time to tackle the kumiko.

Different kinds of top rail

There are three kinds of top rail in use in shoji: *Usu-zan*, *nageshi-zan*, and *maru-zan*.

Usu-zan	Nageshi-zan	Maru-zan
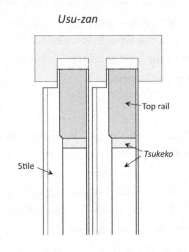	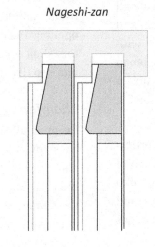	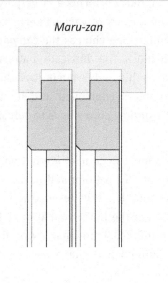
The *usu-zan* is a thinner rail and is the simplest design. There are only two points on the shoji that come into contact with the head jamb as it slides — the left and right stiles at the end — so any slight sagging or slight movement of the head jamb due to age or the effects of earthquakes is less noticeable.	The *nageshi-zan* has a tapered face, and is more attractive and stylish than the *usu-zan*. It has the same advantages as the *usu-zan*. We will tackle this type of rail in the next shoji.	The *maru-zan* is the type I normally use. It forms the most attractive line at the top so it is used with high-quality shoji. However it comes into contact with the groove in the head jamb over its entire width, so any movement of the head jamb is very noticeable, and in installing, there is absolutely no room for error.

Cutting and assembling the kumiko

In the past, the hand saw and chisel were the tools the *tateguya* relied on to cut the kumiko joints for their shoji, and in this fine and detailed work their skills were unsurpassed. Today, though, it's the radial saw, often with computer-controlled mechanisms providing accuracy to 0.01 mm, that performs a large part of this work in Japan. Cutters of various kerf sizes provide all the kumiko size choices the *tateguya* needs, and this includes the intricate pattern work with kumiko as thin as 1.5 mm or less. Outside of Japan the computer-controlled radial saw is not a realistic option, so we have to rely on our sawing skills.

In this shoji, the kumiko are in two sizes: vertical kumiko of 15 x 6.4 mm and horizontal kumiko of 14 x 6.4 mm. For this design, the vertical kumiko sit proud of the horizontal kumiko by 1 mm, and there is a 0.5–0.9 mm chamfer on the front edges of all kumiko and the front inner edge of the *tsukeko*.

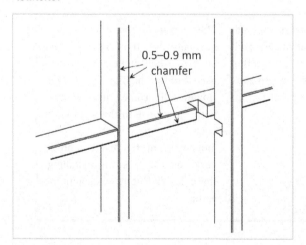

Diagram 77 Kumiko chamfers

This type of joinery is called *men-jiri* (or *men-ochi*). To me, the chamfered edges and 1 mm step between the vertical and horizontal kumiko give the shoji a feeling of style and class, but again, whether to make the kumiko all the one size with no chamfer, or to have different *mikomi* sizes with chamfered edges is a personal choice. Either way, traditionally the vertical kumiko sit on top of the horizontal kumiko.

Another way of cutting the kumiko is with a weave pattern. This is known as *kiri-kaeshi*, and it provides countering forces within the kumiko to prevent the kumiko structure from warping. In most conditions, though, I don't believe this is necessary provided the choice of wood has been sound, the kumiko joints have been properly cut, and the shoji is well made. This type of assembly can often be seen in windows in entrances to traditional Japanese homes where the regular opening and closing of the front door may subject the shoji to significant temperature variations more so than in the inner rooms.

Chamfering

Examine all the kumiko, and select the front and back for each, and separate them into the first and second shoji. The kumiko front should have the cleanest lines. On the back toward one end of the kumiko for the first shoji place a single pencil mark, and two pencil marks on the kumiko for the second shoji. These marks will signify the bottom end for the vertical kumiko, and the left end for the horizontal kumiko.

Photograph 75 Mark backs of kumiko

Using the chamfering jig, chamfer the front of all kumiko, and also the front inner edge of the *tsukeko*. Do not chamfer the back of the kumiko. Do not chamfer the back edges of the *tsukeko*, and the front edge where it joins the main frame.

The chamfer should be about 0.5–0.9 mm, which is a couple of strokes of the plane. To avoid the possibility of chamfering below the line of the intersecting kumiko, chamfer at a slightly shallower angle than 45°. Place the *tsukeko* safely out of the way with the rails and stiles. After they have been chamfered, square off the ends of the kumiko.

Photograph 76 Chamfer kumiko

Vertical kumiko

Clamp one of the vertical kumiko to the story stick, making sure that the kumiko is correctly oriented with the top and bottom of the story stick. Transfer the marks from the story stick to the back of the kumiko with a sharp marking knife. Remove the kumiko and mark the ends of the 13 mm tenons separately. Extend the tenon shoulder and tenon end marks around to the front side of the kumiko. Mark the cheeks of the tenons according to the following diagram.

Vertical kumiko

Back (paper side)

4.3

6.4   15   7.5

6.4

13

Diagram 78 Vertical kumiko dimensions

Clamp the six vertical kumiko to the side support in the kumiko cutting jig (Page 60) with their backs up (chamfer facing down — pencil marks

visible) and the ends firmly butted up against the end stop on the jig. Group the kumiko by shoji number. In this case, I always place the previously marked kumiko against the side support.

From the previously marked kumiko, mark the tenon shoulders and ends, and the kumiko joint positions on all kumiko. Mark the near side kumiko with the tenon cheeks.

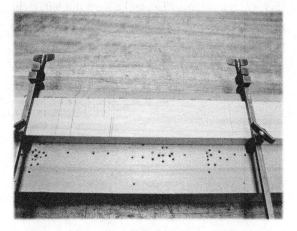

Photograph 77 Secure kumiko in the cutting jig

With the fine-tooth cross-cut saw, cut all kumiko marks to a depth of 7.5 mm, ensuring that the depth of cut is consistent for all kumiko. Flip the jig around and mark and cut the other side of the kumiko half-lap joint as you did in the exercise on Pages 67–69. Remove the waste.

Cut the tenon shoulders and tenon ends down to the cheek line and remove the waste. Unclamp the kumiko and flip over so the front (chamfered) side is facing up, clamp the kumiko to the side support and make sure the ends with the mark are butted firmly up against the end stop. Extend the tenon shoulder and tenon end marks across all kumiko, cut down to the tenon cheek marks, and remove the waste.

Photograph 78 Cut tenons and remove waste

Remove the kumiko from the jig, and cut the tenons off at the ends. Chamfer the ends of the tenons.

Horizontal kumiko

Repeat exactly the same procedure above for the horizontal kumiko. The horizontal kumiko are cut on the front (chamfered) side so be mindful of this when marking. Also, make sure the left/right orientation is correct when marking the kumiko from the story stick.

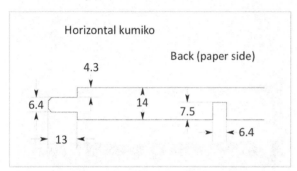

Horizontal kumiko

Back (paper side)

4.3

6.4   14   7.5

13   6.4

Diagram 79 Horizontal kumiko dimensions

Assembling

Group the kumiko by shoji number, and assemble. Make sure the kumiko are in their correct orientation — the vertical kumiko pencil marks should be on the bottom, and the horizontal kumiko pencil marks should be on the left. Add a small dab of white PVA glue to the sides of the half-lap joints (not the bottoms) in the horizontal kumiko, then insert the vertical kumiko.

Photograph 79 Add glue to sides of joints

When assembling, push the vertical kumiko down into the horizontal kumiko lightly. It should go in with a slight amount of tension. If there is some resistance, stop pushing with your fingers, as the kumiko could snap. Tap the joint lightly with the *gennō* and hardwood block. It should go together with a couple of light taps.

If the joints were too tight and you had to force them together with the *gennō* and hardwood block, you'll notice that the kumiko will bow upwards. If so, flip the completed kumiko assembly over and place a moderate weight in the center while the glue dries. This won't completely fix the problem, but it will help to a small degree.

Dab a small amount of glue into the mortises in the horizontal *tsukeko*, and attach to the kumiko assembly, making sure you have the correct left/right orientation.

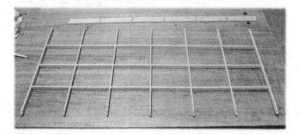

Photograph 80 Attach horizontal *tsukeko*

Now dab glue into the vertical *tsukeko* mortises and attach to the kumiko assembly. If you prefer, you can hammer in a thin tack or nail through the miter joint from the horizontal *tsukeko* side for a tight fit, but make sure you drill an appropriately sized pilot hole for the nail to prevent the joint from splitting.

Check the miters, and use a small plane to make the faces flush if necessary. Place the completed kumiko assembly safely to one side.

Photograph 81 Attach vertical *tsukeko* to complete assembly

Planing the rails and stiles

If you are using a *kanna* for the final planing, make sure the sole is properly conditioned and you sharpen the blade to the highest grit sharpening stone you have available. Plane all sides of the rails and stiles to give the timber a polished glistening appearance. Lightly chamfer all edges except the front inside edge with your normal *kanna*.

Chamfer the front inner edges of the rails with the *kakumen-ganna* exactly as you did in the exercise. Without adjusting the *kanna* setting, chamfer the inner front edges of the stiles. The shoji is now ready to assemble.

Assembling the shoji

Spread a very thin film of glue along the outer sides of the top and bottom (horizontal) *tsukeko*, then dab a small amount of glue in the mortises in the top and bottom rails and insert the assembled kumiko. Make sure all pieces are correctly oriented, and tap the rails lightly if necessary using the *gennō* and hardwood block so the kumiko tenons are fully seated.

Now comes the moment of truth. Spread a thin film of glue along the outer sides of the vertical *tsukeko*, and apply glue to all the stile mortises, including those for the kumiko and *tsukeko*. With the stile resting on a clean and solid surface, insert one side of the rail tenons into the corresponding stile mortises, and carefully tap down with the *gennō* and hardwood block until the kumiko tenons begin to enter the mortises. Repeat this with the other stile.

Once the kumiko tenons have started to enter the mortises you can then hit the frame with slightly more force. The tenons are 1 mm wider than the mortises so you will need to use a reasonable amount of strength with the *gennō*. Hit up and down the stiles along their full length so the tenons enter evenly, and continually monitor the condition of the kumiko as they enter their mortises. If necessary, flip the piece over and tap along the other stile.

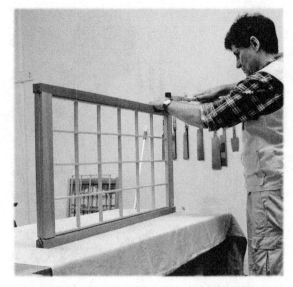

Photograph 82 Tap in stiles with a *gennō* and hardwood block

As the *jaguchi* on the rails begin to reach near the chamfers on the stiles, reduce the level of force, and closely observe these parts as they come together. When the tenons fit tightly and the *jaguchi* have mated with the chamfers firmly, quickly check the condition of the joints, make sure the outer sides of the *tsukeko* are in full and flush contact with the rails and stiles, and wipe away any glue that has squeezed out.

Sight down the face of the shoji from the top and side to check there's no twist, and use the large try square to check that the shoji is square. Make any minor adjustments by twisting or tapping as necessary. Place the completed shoji to one side for the glue to dry, and start on the second shoji, following exactly the same procedure.

When the shoji have dried thoroughly, inspect the join between the *jaguchi* and the chamfers in the top and bottom rails, and plane flush with the stile if required (Photograph 83). This should only take a couple of very light shavings.

93

Photograph 83 Clean up joints with the *kanna*

Mark the location of the door pulls on the stiles as shown in Diagram 64 on page 77 and cut out the housing mortise. Be careful not to mar the face of the shoji. This step can be done before applying water to raise the grain if you prefer, but the pull should not be inserted at that time.

Photograph 84 Mortise for pull

Apply a small dab of glue to the mortise, and insert the pull so that it sits flush with the face.

Photograph 85 Pull sits flush with the face

Attaching the paper

This is the final procedure before installation. Lay a blanket or some other protective covering over your workbench so you do not mark the face of the shoji. Mix the starch glue to a smooth and even creamy consistency. Using the brush (called a *hake* in Japan), apply the starch glue to the backs of the *tsukeko* and kumiko with a patting action — do not wipe or scrape as the glue is likely to run down the sides (*mikomi*) of the kumiko.

Photograph 86 Apply glue with a patting action

If any glue goes on to the kumiko *mikomi* face wipe it off thoroughly before attaching the paper. Be careful to avoid getting the glue on the stiles and rails.

Rest the roll of paper across the stiles at the bottom part of the shoji with the bottom edge of the paper extending about 100 mm past the bottom *tsukeko*. Place a length of wood with chamfered edges on the bottom part of the paper to stop it from moving. The roll of paper will sit across the stiles 3 mm above the kumiko, so there is no fear that the paper will contact the glue until it is unrolled.

This is strictly a "one-go" operation, as once the paper contacts the glue, it should not be moved. Roll out the paper slowly from the bottom of the shoji with the sides parallel to the line of the stiles and flatten down on to the glue carefully with your open hand as you unroll the paper, spreading from the center to the outer sides.

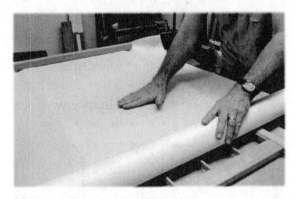

Photograph 87 Spread out the shoji paper

When the paper is unrolled past the top rail, cut the paper off with a cutter, taking care not to mark or scratch the shoji frame. Also cut along the outer sides to remove the side overhang.

With the tips of your fingers and fingernails, press the paper into the edges where the *tsukeko* and rails and stiles join, gently pulling the paper out at the same time.

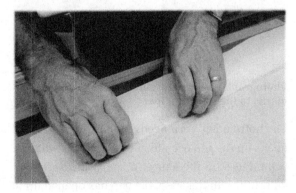

Photograph 88 Press paper into edges

Once the paper is attached to the kumiko and *tsukeko*, place the metal straightedge along the *tsukeko* and cut the paper along the line where the *tsukeko* joins the rails and stiles (a wide paint

scraper also works well). Make sure the cutter has a new edge and is very sharp. The paper along the cutting line is moist with the glue, so the cutter blade should be extended a reasonable amount and the angle of cut should be quite low. If the blade is not sharp or the angle of cut is too high, the cutter will tend to tear the paper rather than cut.

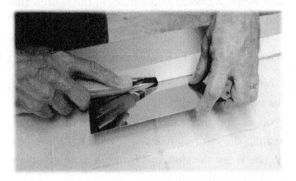

Photograph 89 Trim paper to fit

The corners can be slightly difficult to cut cleanly at times so work carefully in these areas. After cutting the paper, carefully wipe off any glue from the rails and stiles, making sure the cloth does not touch the paper.

When the glue on both shoji has dried thoroughly, lightly mist the back of the paper with clean water using the atomizer. The fibers in the paper will shrink as they dry, making the paper taut.

Fitting and adjusting the shoji

This is the final step where all the previous care and effort comes to fruition. In a perfect world all door and window frames are square, and all we need to do is cut the rebates on the stiles for a flawless fit and smooth sliding shoji. Unfortunately, reality is rarely this kind, and shoji will usually require some level of adjustment to fit. This is why the 5 mm and 10 mm horns have been left on the stiles.

If this procedure is not approached systematically, you will more than likely keep cutting off small amounts from the left horn, then the right horn, then the left, right, left and right again until frustration sets in and you find you've cut off too much. The following is the way I was taught at

Shokugei Gakuin, and it ensures that the sides of the shoji line up with the pillars quickly and with minimal cuts. Minor adjustment at the end can then be done with a few strokes of the *kanna*.

In a two panel shoji set, the left-hand shoji sits to the rear, and the right-hand shoji to the front. This is also the order for a three panel set; for a four panel set where they meet in the center, the order is taken from the house entrance (*genkan*) — from the *genkan* side the two inner shoji are to the front, and the two outer shoji are to the rear.

First, adjust the left-hand shoji. Rest the bottom of the horns on the outside ledge of the bottom track grooves and place the left-hand side of the shoji against the left pillar or frame. Check if there is a gap between the shoji and frame, and whether it's at the top or bottom.

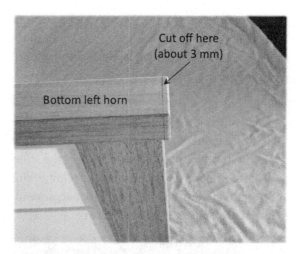

Photograph 91 Trim from the bottom left horn

Trim about 3 mm from the bottom left horn. The horn is 5 mm long, so this leaves about 2 mm, which will fit in the 3 mm deep groove and conceal the bottom of the rail by about 1 mm.

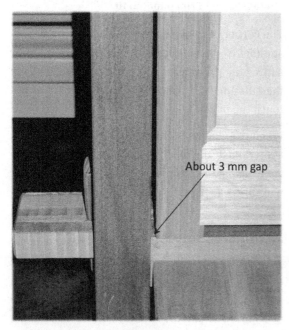

Photograph 90 Gap at bottom

In the left-hand shoji, there is a gap at the bottom of roughly 3 mm. The first thing to do is resist the temptation to immediately trim the bottom of the right-hand stile to try to square it up. Start from the left-hand side and open the gap more (if the gap is at the top, start on the right-hand side).

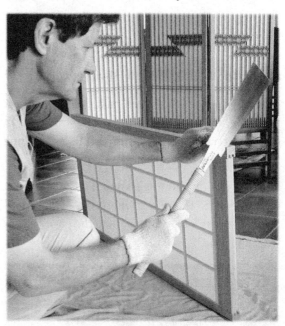

Photograph 92 Work carefully to avoid damage or marks to the shoji or paper

The bottom left horn needs no more cutting. This opens up the gap even further, but this is what we want. Measure the gap — a rough measurement will suffice. In this case, the gap has opened up to about 9–10 mm.

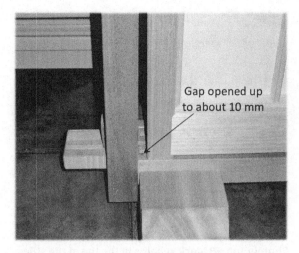

Photograph 93 Wider gap at the bottom

Halve that gap measurement — about 5 mm — and trim that amount from the bottom right horn.

Photograph 94 Trim bottom right horn

If the cutting has been accurate, the left-hand side of the shoji should now sit flush with the frame on the left. Any minor adjustment necessary can be done with a couple of strokes of the *kanna*. In this case, two strokes of the *kanna* on the bottom of the right horn had the left-hand side sitting perfectly flush with the left pillar.

Photograph 95 Minor adjustment with the *kanna*

Extend the rebate line on the bottom rail to the two stiles, and cut out the rebate on the stiles.

Photograph 96 Cut the rebates in the bottom of the stiles

97

Clean up the stile rebates with the *kiwa-ganna* or shoulder plane so they are flush with the rail rebate and they fit into the groove. Lightly plane the shoulder of the rebate on the right-hand side if necessary so the entire rebate line is parallel to the bottom track line.

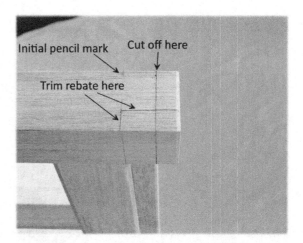

Photograph 97 Clean up the rebates with the *kiwa-ganna*

Place the bottom of the shoji in the front groove to check that the left-hand side is still flush with the left-hand pillar, and that the shoji slides smoothly in the groove all the way across.

If all is well, chamfer around the bottom of the stiles, and lightly chamfer the rebate lines.

Put the shoji back on the front ledge of the bottom track and place the top against the top track. Make a light pencil mark on the back of the each of the stiles where they meet the track. This indicates the top rebate shoulder mark. Measure up about 14 mm and cut off the horns at those second marks. Cut out rebates in the front of the stiles down to the rebate shoulder mark.

Photograph 98 Mark rebates in the top of the stiles

If the rebate shoulder mark on the stile is above the existing rebate on the rail, cut the rebate so it is even with the rail rebate. If it is below the existing rail rebate, the rail rebate will need to be trimmed to that mark. Clean up the stile rebates with the *kiwa-ganna* or shoulder plane so they are flush with the rail rebate and they fit into the groove.

Insert the shoji into its groove (left shoji in the rear groove). If it doesn't go in easily, check whether the top or the rebate needs to be adjusted. Do not trim the bottom horns.

Check that the top rebate line along the width of the shoji is parallel to the top track, and lightly plane the rebate shoulder where necessary; it is very noticeable if these two lines are not parallel, especially at the top.

Photograph 99 Parallel lines and tight-fitting joints

Check again that the left side sits flush with the left-hand side frame, and that the shoji runs smoothly all the way across. Chamfer around the top horns, and lightly chamfer the rebate lines.

Photograph 100 Left-hand panel completed

Remove the shoji, and follow this procedure exactly with the right-hand shoji, but this time you'll need to make sure it sits flush against the right-hand side of the door or window frame.

Photograph 101 Project completed

Making a *KASUMI-GUMI* Shoji

Photograph 102 *Kasumi-gumi koshitsuki-shōji*

In this section I'll explain how to make a *ko-shitsuki-shōji* with a *kasumi-gumi* kumiko pattern. *Kasumi* is the Japanese word for mist, and through the use of shorter and thinner horizontal kumiko, the *kasumi-gumi* pattern gives the feeling of a light mist settling around the shoji. It is a popular pattern for *shoin-shōji* where a more complex pattern perhaps might be too expensive, or simply not to the owner's liking.

A vast array of expressions are possible with the *kasumi* pattern simply by increasing or decreasing the number of vertical or horizontal kumiko,

and altering how the horizontal *kasumi* kumiko are arranged; for example, the *kasumi* kumiko can be made progressively longer or shorter as in the bottom section of the shoji above, or they can alternate between the left and right sides, or they can be cut short and laid out to form zigzag or other patterns. The variations are limitless.

The hip-board at the bottom adds a sense of strength and stability, and to avoid the feeling of the shoji being too bottom-heavy, I've reduced the width of the bottom rail from 60 mm (as in the previous shoji) to 45 mm, the same width as the top rail.

The kumiko are joined in exactly the same way as the previous shoji, i.e. half-lap housing joints connecting the horizontal and vertical kumiko, however, the *mitsuke* of the horizontal *kasumi* kumiko is narrower than the other kumiko (4.0 mm compared to 6.4 mm), and they sit proud of the vertical kumiko. This means that the vertical kumiko will have to be cut on the front and back, and because the *kasumi* kumiko don't extend all the way across, in many cases the vertical kumiko can't be cut as a single group — kumiko will have to be added and removed as required when cutting.

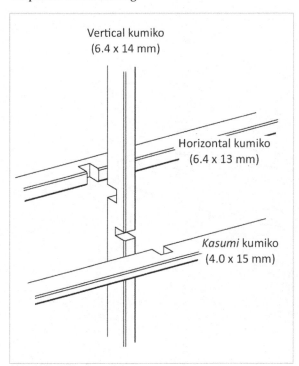

Diagram 80 Kumiko joinery details

Another point to note is that the two shoji panels are a mirror image of each other, and this poses an additional challenge when marking and cutting the kumiko. There is, however, a simple method to overcome this difficulty, and I'll explain this in the kumiko assembly section.

These variations in half-lap placement and size make this much more difficult than the previous shoji, and care and concentration is essential.

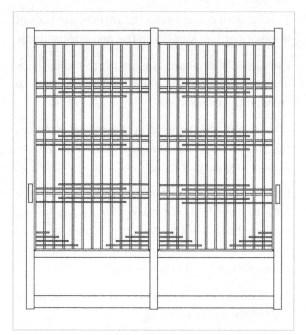

Diagram 81 The two shoji panels are a mirror image

Jigs

45° jig

This jig is used to cut even chamfers in the ends of the short *kasumi* kumiko on the two sides and top.

Each kumiko is placed up against the inner side, and a block plane runs along the two 45° faces to chamfer the edges at 45°.

This jig will also be used in the next shoji to cut the end angles for the *asa-no-ha* and *izutsu-tsunagi* kumiko patterns.

I used two layers of MDF for both sides and the base to give the block plane a broad supporting surface. I also attached a 20 x 20 mm piece of wood on the bottom so I could secure the jig in my workbench vise when in use.

For the later kumiko patterns in particular, make sure the angle is exactly 45°

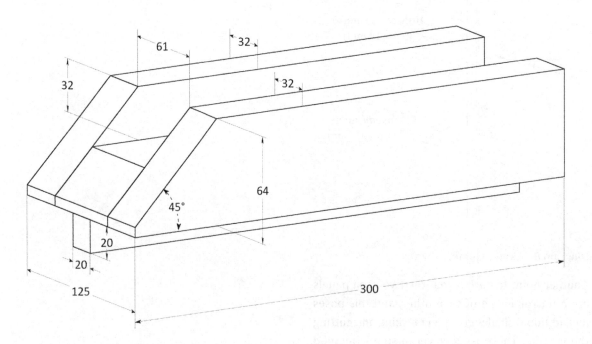

Diagram 82 45° jig

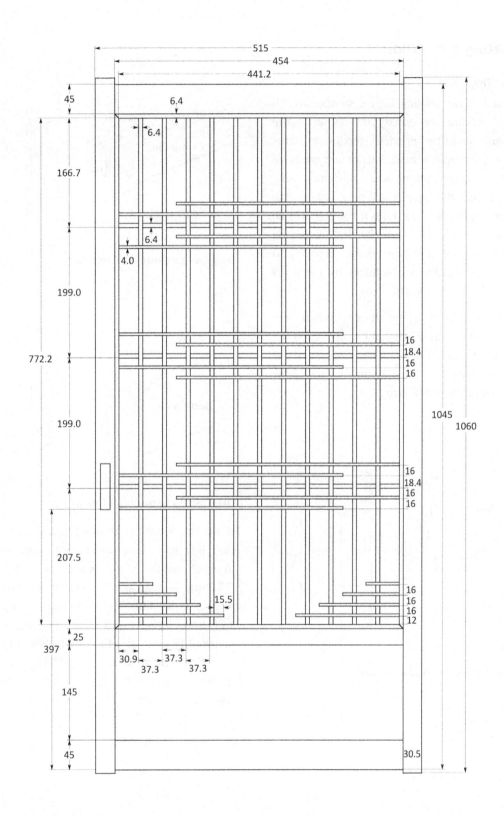

Diagram 83 Shoji dimension details

103

Calculating dimensions

Overall shoji size

I'll use the same holding frame, so the overall shoji dimensions are exactly the same as the *mizugoshi-shōji* in the previous section, but this time I'll use a couple of variations so you can have a greater range of options when designing your own shoji. Here the top rail will be a *nageshi-zan* so you can gain a feel for how it compares with the *maru-zan* style I used in the first shoji (see Page 89); instead of a *jaguchi*, the center and bottom rails and stiles will be joined by a *men-jiri* join; and I'll add a hip-board.

Moreover, in this shoji I've decided not to use haunches in the bottom rails, so I've increased the width of the tenons. The following diagrams show the joinery (note that the diagrams do not show the grooves for the hip-board).

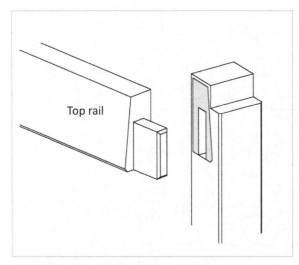

Diagram 84 *Nageshi-zan* for top rail

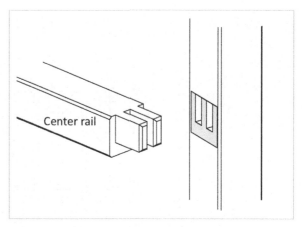

Diagram 85 Center rail tenons

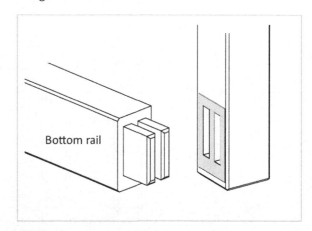

Diagram 86 Bottom rail tenons

While the overall shoji dimensions are the same, the internal dimensions are different. The internal width is the same at 441.2 (515 – 73.8 mm — see Page 77), but the internal height is 1045 mm minus the widths of the top, center and bottom rails (45 + 25 + 45 mm), the hip-board (145 mm), and the two *tsukeko* (12.8 mm), so the calculation is 1045 – 115 – 145 – 12.8 = 772.2 mm. The internal space is therefore 441.2 x 772.2 mm.

Kumiko calculations

The vertical kumiko are spaced evenly so the horizontal calculations are simply $441.2 + 6.4 = 447.6$; there are 11 vertical kumiko so 12 intervals, therefore $447.6 \div 12 = 37.3$ mm pitch.

The horizontal kumiko consist of two different sized *mitsuke*, and kumiko formed into groups, so rather than using an equation to calculate intervals, we need to aim at achieving a visual balance. In this design I decided on an interval between grouped horizontal kumiko of 12.0 mm, or a pitch of 16 mm between 4.0 mm kumiko, and 18.4 mm between 6.4 and 4.0 mm kumiko.

Working out the intervals between kumiko groups was simply a matter of trial and error until I achieved what I thought was a reasonable balance.

Using trial and error to obtain an acceptable balance for the more complex and non-uniform kumiko arrangements is a normal part of shoji pattern design. An "acceptable balance" is largely subjective, but one principle I adhere to is that while individual kumiko within groups can be positioned quite close together, there should be sufficient space between groups so they do not become too cramped. This applies to this shoji, and also to the *kawari-gumi* shoji we make next.

The dimensions I eventually settled on are shown in Diagram 83 (Page 103).

Preparing the timber

Milling

The principles for timber selection described in the previous shoji also apply to this shoji.

The stiles are the same as the previous shoji, however both the top and bottom rails are different, and there's a hip-board and an additional rail for the hip-board.

I've decided to give the hip-board a horizontal orientation to maintain the overall flow of the two shoji themselves. A strong grain pattern here will give the shoji considerable interest. The milling requirements are therefore as follows.

Cutting List (in millimeters)

Component	L	W	T	N
Top rail	550	45	21	2
Bottom rail	550	45	27	2
Center rail	550	25	27	2
Stile	1,110	30.5	30.5	4
Hip-board	550	156	8	2
Vertical kumiko	850	6.4	14	25
Horizontal kumiko	550	6.4	13	7
Kasumi kumiko	550	4.0	15	33
Tsukeko	1,100	6.4	16	6
Story stick	1,300	20	20	1

L: Length (cut oversize); W: Width (*mitsuke*); T: Thickness (*mikomi*); N: Number (this is the minimum number required)

Table 3 *Kasumi-gumi* shoji cutting list

The taper on the top rail is from 16 mm at the top to 21 mm at the bottom (see Diagram 92 on Page 107).

Marking

Follow exactly the same marking process as in the previous shoji (from Page 80).

Story stick

Mark the story stick with all stile, rail and kumiko markings with a sharp marking knife. You will notice that the *kasumi* kumiko in the three upper groups do not extend all the way across, and note that the kumiko order in the center group is different from that in the top and bottom groups.

For the three upper groups, you will need to mark the main horizontal kumiko first, then the *kasumi* kumiko in their respective groups measured from the main horizontal kumiko.

Mark the *kasumi* kumiko on the story stick with an asterisk or some other mark to remind you to take care when marking the left and right stiles and *tsukeko*, and because there are many more kumiko than in the previous shoji, number each of the horizontal and vertical kumiko joints so you can keep track of their correct order when cutting. Number the vertical kumiko marks from the left (or use letters), and all horizontal kumiko including the *kasumi* kumiko marks from the bottom. These numbers will be vital to keep track of the cuts and kumiko placement (see Diagram 98 on Page 110).

Stiles

Mark the mortise locations on all stiles as shown in the following diagrams. Trim the ends of the stiles at the horn marks, and chamfer around the top and bottom edges. In this shoji there is no need for tenons on the *tsukeko*, so *tsukeko* mortises are not required.

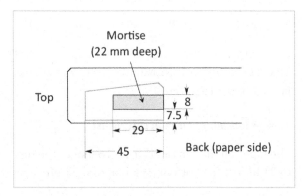

Diagram 87 Stile mortise positions – top

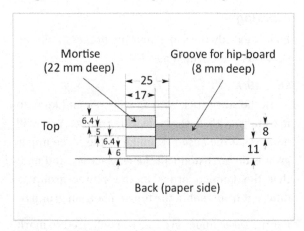

Diagram 88 Stile mortise and groove positions – center

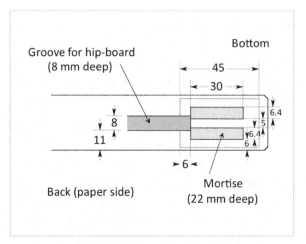

Diagram 89 Stile mortise and groove positions – bottom

As with the previous shoji, the backs of the horizontal kumiko and *kasumi* kumiko are 3 mm from the back of the stile, so the kumiko mortises for both types are positioned 7.3 mm from the back of the stile.

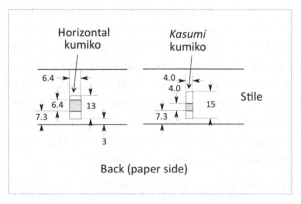

Diagram 90 Stile mortise positions – kumiko

The stiles and vertical *tsukeko* are the pieces where errors in kumiko marking are most likely to occur. If you look carefully at Photograph 102 and Diagram 81, you will notice that the markings for the two outer stiles (and vertical *tsukeko*) are the same, and the two inner stiles (and vertical *tsukeko*) are the same, so use this to confirm that your vertical stile and *tsukeko* marks are in the correct position.

Mark the position of the grooves for the hip-board as shown in Diagrams 88 and 89. These are 11 mm from the back, and 8 mm wide.

Rails

Mark the tenons and mortise locations on the rails as shown in the following diagrams. Remember that the rails do not have the *jaguchi* extension, so mark their tenon shoulders all the way around. Also note that the top rail has a single tenon, while the center and bottom rails have double tenons.

As with the previous shoji, the backs of the vertical kumiko are 1.5 mm from the back of the rail, so the kumiko mortises are cut 5.8 mm from the back.

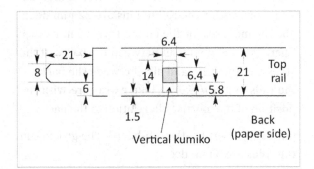

Diagram 91 Top rail tenons and mortise positions

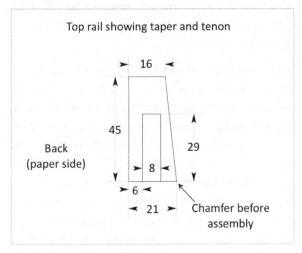

Diagram 92 Top rail tenons and taper

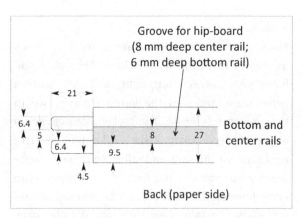

Diagram 93 Center and bottom rail tenons and groove positions

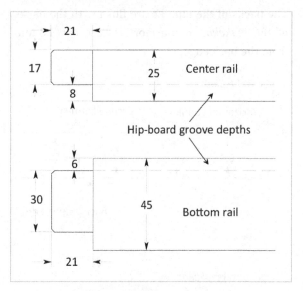

Diagram 94 Center and bottom rail tenons

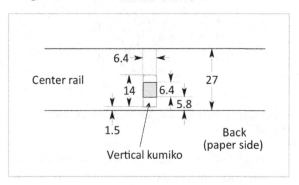

Diagram 95 Center rail kumiko mortise position

Mark the position of the grooves in the bottom and center rails for the hip-board as shown in Diagram 93. These are 9.5 mm from the back and 8 mm wide.

Make sure that the kumiko mortises are marked on the upper side of the center rail and the groove is marked on the lower side.

Tsukeko

Mark the mortises for the kumiko on the *tsukeko* as shown in Diagram 96 below. Make sure you have the correct left/right and top/bottom orientation, and that the kumiko marks are in their correct position. The *tsukeko* can cover up any errors you may make in kumiko mortise positions on the rails and stiles, so there is some leeway, but not with mortises in the *tsukeko* — an error here on the *tsukeko* can't be covered up and will show, so take your time and double-check each mark.

The backs of the kumiko are flush with the backs of the *tsukeko*, so the mortises are cut 4.3 mm from the back edge.

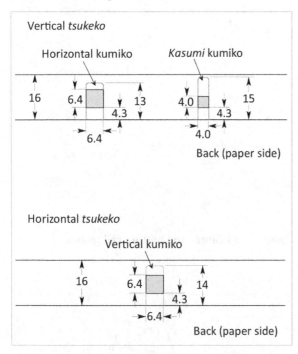

Diagram 96 Vertical and horizontal *tsukeko* mortises

Although some of the purists may disagree, in this kumiko arrangement there's really no need for the complex joint in the *tsukeko* miters that was required in the previous shoji. The kumiko are quite close to the rails and stiles, so the kumiko tenons through the *tsukeko* into the rails/stiles combined with small tacks or nails driven into the miters from the vertical *tsukeko* sides give the miters all the strength they need. Therefore, simply cut and trim the ends at 45° to the required mark on the 45° shooting board.

Hip-board

The final dimensions for the hip-boards are 468 x 156 mm. This allows 3 mm of wood movement within the grooves across the width and 2 mm across the length of the hip-boards. This should be sufficient for most timbers.

Cutting the frames

Mortises, tenons and grooves

Stiles

Cut out the mortises for the rail tenons and kumiko in the stiles using your preferred method. The mortises for the rail tenons are 22 mm deep, and the mortises for the kumiko are 7.5 mm deep. There is a 1.5 mm offset between the backs of the stiles and the rails, and also between the backs of the rails and *tsukeko*, so take extra care with the position of the mortises in relation to the back.

Cut the grooves for the hip-board. The grooves in the stiles are 8 mm deep.

Rails

Cut the tenons to the dimensions specified in Diagrams 91–94. Cut the mortises for the kumiko to a depth of 7.5 mm.

Once you have cut the mortises, and if you didn't do so earlier, cut the taper in the top rail. This can be done on the table-saw, bandsaw, or by hand using a plane. If you decide to use a table-saw or bandsaw, make sure you follow all the necessary safety precautions, as this can be a dangerous cut. My preferred method and the method I recommend, especially considering safety, is to trim the taper by hand with a plane. For the tapered rails in this shoji, I used two *kanna* (one set for a slightly coarser cut and one set for a fine cut), and each taper took me no more than five minutes to cut.

Cut the grooves for the hip-board in the bottom and center rails. Note that the groove depth is 8 mm on the center rail, but 6 mm on the bottom rail. This gives a 3 mm space in the center rail groove for wood movement.

Finally, chamfer the ends of the tenons, and cut the hip-board to the correct size (468 x 156 mm).

Tsukeko

Cut the mortises in the *tsukeko*. These are through mortises, so make sure the back face where the mortise came through is clean of waste.

Rebates

For the rail and stile joinery used in this shoji, you only need to cut a rebate in the bottom rail. The dimensions for this rebate are exactly the same as in the previous shoji — it is cut 19.5 mm from the back to a depth of 4 mm. As was the case in the previous shoji, the rebates in the stiles are cut on-site.

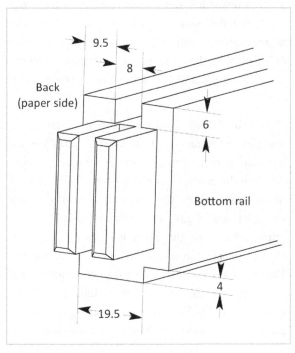

Diagram 97 Bottom rail rebate

Raising the grain

Place the *tsukeko* safely to one side. Thoroughly wet a piece of cloth and wipe the water liberally over the rails and stiles, then place to one side and allow to dry.

This completes work on the frames until the pre-assembly step, and it's now time to tackle the kumiko.

Cutting and assembling the kumiko

This shoji presents a challenge when cutting the kumiko because none of the *kasumi* kumiko extend across the entire width of the shoji. To reduce the possibility of error when cutting the vertical kumiko, the following simple kumiko and joint numbering and lettering system can be used for this shoji.

This numbering system is only a suggestion; if you prefer a different way, then by all means use that, as long as you understand it and it works. Personally, I prefer to use only numbers for both vertical and horizontal kumiko, but I realize this can become somewhat confusing, especially when making this shoji for the first time, so this combined numbering and lettering system might be the better option in the early stages.

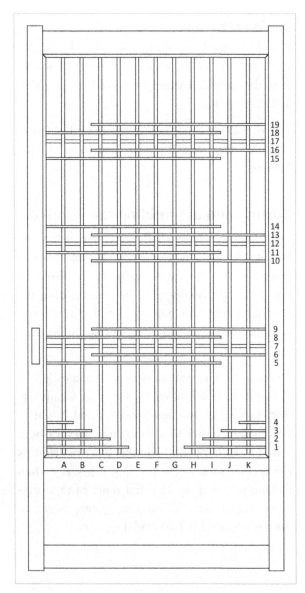

Diagram 98 Suggested numbering system – left shoji

Using the chamfering jig, chamfer the fronts of all kumiko, and also the front inner edge of the *tsukeko*. Do not chamfer the back of the kumiko. Do not chamfer the back edges of the *tsukeko*, and the front edge where it joins the main frame.

This chamfer should be about 0.5–0.9 mm, which is a couple of strokes of the plane. To avoid the possibility of chamfering below the line of the intersecting kumiko, chamfer at a slightly shallower angle than 45° (see Photograph 76 on Page 91). Place the *tsukeko* safely out of the way with the rails and stiles. After they have been chamfered, square off the ends of the kumiko.

Vertical kumiko

Cutting the vertical kumiko presents somewhat of a challenge. Cuts need to be made on both the front and the back, and the cuts for the *kasumi* kumiko on the front are in different positions for different kumiko. The use of a master vertical kumiko for each shoji makes this process much easier.

Clamp the master kumiko to the story stick and transfer all tenon and horizontal and *kasumi* kumiko marks with a sharp marking knife. Remove the master kumiko and mark the ends of the 13 mm tenons separately. Extend the tenon shoulder and tenon end marks around to the opposite side of the master kumiko. Mark the cheeks of the tenons according to Diagram 99. These master kumiko — one for each shoji — are the ones you use for marking and cutting all vertical kumiko. They remain in the jig as you cut the vertical kumiko for their respective shoji.

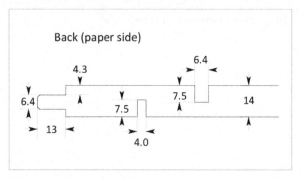

Diagram 99 Vertical kumiko joinery

Similar to the previous shoji, the vertical kumiko sit proud of the horizontal kumiko by 1 mm, but in this shoji, the horizontal *kasumi* kumiko are then fitted and sit proud of the vertical kumiko by 1 mm, as shown in Diagram 80 on Page 101. As before, there is a 0.5–0.9 mm chamfer on the front edges of all kumiko, and the front inner edge of the *tsukeko*.

Chamfering

Examine all the kumiko, and select the front and back for each. Mark the back of the kumiko with pencil as explained in the previous shoji.

110

First, place all 11 vertical kumiko with their backs up (chamfer facing down) and one of the master kumiko in the jig, making sure that the ends of all the kumiko are firmly against the end stop. Mark and cut the three 6.4 mm horizontal kumiko half-lap joints (7, 12, and 17), and the tenons.

Photograph 103 Mark and cut the backs

Once the back joints and tenons have been cut, flip the kumiko over and cut the tenons on the front. DO NOT cut off the ends of the tenons at this stage.

Photograph 104 Cut the tenons, and the joints for the horizontal kumiko on the back

If you find that cutting all eleven kumiko at the same time is too difficult or will affect accuracy, cut five then six separately. You will, however, have to make up an extra master vertical kumiko for this.

All additional cuts on the vertical kumiko will now be on the front (chamfer facing up) at 4.0 mm.

Starting from the bottom, place vertical kumiko A, B, C, D, H, I, J and K in the jig with the master kumiko, and cut the joint for the first horizontal joint (1), which is for the first *kasumi* kumiko (4 mm).

Photograph 105 Cut the first *kasumi* kumiko joint in the bottom group

Place kumiko A, B, C, I, J and K in the jig and cut joint 2; kumiko A, B, J and K and cut joint 3; then kumiko A and K and cut joint 4. That completes the bottom group.

When cleaning the waste from the cut, make sure that both sides of the joint are fully supported, especially when the joints are as close as they are on this shoji, to prevent any damage to the kumiko.

Photograph 106 Make sure both sides of the joint are fully supported when removing the waste

Place kumiko A – I inclusive in the jig with the master kumiko and cut joints 5, 8, 11, 14, 15 and 18. Then place kumiko C – K inclusive in the jig with the master kumiko and cut joints 6, 9, 10, 13, 16 and 19.

Photograph 107 Make sure the correct cuts are made on the correct kumiko

Cut off the ends of the tenons and chamfer as was done in the previous shoji.

Horizontal kumiko

The horizontal kumiko are quite straightforward. They are cut on the front (chamfer up), and because there are only three in each shoji, join the two sets and cut all joints A–K on all six at the one time. Cut the tenons, remove the waste, and chamfer the ends.

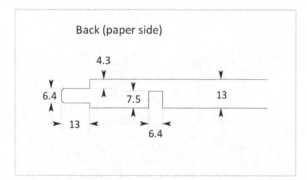

Diagram 100 Horizontal kumiko joinery

Photograph 108 Horizontal kumiko are cut on the front

Kasumi kumiko

The *kasumi* kumiko are also quite straightforward. They are cut on the back so the chamfer is facing down. Although the *kasumi* kumiko vary, the easiest way is to cut the 16 together for all half-lap joints A–K. Once this is done, cut the tenons, remove the waste and chamfer the ends as with all other kumiko.

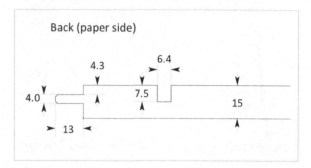

Diagram 101 *Kasumi* kumiko joinery

Cut the *kasumi* kumiko to their proper length as shown in Diagram 83, making sure you keep the correct left/right orientation. Be mindful that the *kasumi* kumiko tenons are at the opposite ends in the right-hand shoji.

Square off the edges, and lightly chamfer the top and two sides, but not the back, using the 45° jig as shown in the following photographs.

Photograph 109 Chamfer the sides then the top with the block plane and 45° jig

Photograph 110 A clean chamfer on three sides

Chamfering all the ends such as this signifies a heightened attention to detail, and conveys a sense of quality and craftsmanship, so I strongly urge that you do not take any shortcuts here.

Assembling

Since the two shoji panels are a mirror image of each other, this poses an interesting challenge. Provided you numbered the vertical kumiko as I recommended, though, the solution is very simple.

On the first shoji panel, position the vertical kumiko from the left from A to K. For the second shoji panel, it's simply a matter of reversing this; position them from the left from K to A. The left/right and bottom/top kumiko orientation must, however, remain the same. Only the vertical kumiko numbers (letters) are reversed for the second shoji.

First assemble the eleven vertical and three horizontal kumiko.

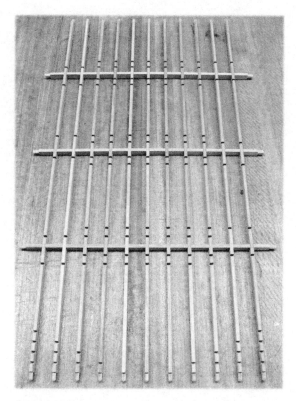

Photograph 111 Start with the vertical and horizontal kumiko

The bottom group is as good a place as any to start with the *kasumi* kumiko. Work slowly and carefully. The *kasumi* kumiko are quite narrow, and can snap easily, especially the longer pieces, so when inserting them into the joints in the vertical kumiko, lightly push them down with your fingers until they become engaged in the joints, then tap them down the rest of the way with a *gennō* and hardwood block. This helps to avoid placing too much pressure on one particular spot.

Photograph 112 Start the *kasumi* kumiko from the bottom

From the bottom group, progressively work your way up the shoji, making sure that the left/right orientation is correct.

Photograph 113 Complete the *kasumi* kumiko then attach the *tsukeko*

Once you have inserted all *kasumi* kumiko, attach the *tsukeko*. As I mentioned earlier, not one for the purists, but in this case a tack or nail through the miters in the *tsukeko* from the stile side will suffice because of the high number of through tenons that will go into the rails and stiles.

Photograph 114 In this case, a tack through the miter from the stile side will suffice

As there are a considerable number of kumiko very close to each other, some very small gaps may appear between the kumiko and *tsukeko*.

Don't be overly concerned about these gaps, because they should close up once the rails and stiles are attached and joined.

Planing the rails and stiles

Plane all sides of the rails and stiles and both faces of the hip-board to give the timber a polished glistening appearance.

Lightly chamfer the back inner edge of the stiles with your normal plane.

Set your chamfer plane to cut a roughly 2 mm chamfer, and chamfer the front inner and two outer edges of the stiles. Provided your marking and cutting has been accurate, this should take the chamfer down to where the rail meets the stile.

Take care with this as cutting too much chamfer will leave an untidy join. If necessary, you can make minor adjustments by planing the front of the rail.

Photograph 115 Carefully chamfer to the point where the rail meets the stile

With the same chamfer setting, chamfer both front edges of the center rails, and the inner front edge of the bottom rails. Lightly chamfer all other edges with your normal plane.

Chamfer the inner front edge of the top rail. The size of the chamfer can vary depending on the feeling you want to convey — a smaller chamfer will increase the "set-back" of the *tsukeko* relative to the front edge of the rail. In this example, I set the chamfer at about 3 mm. Do not chamfer too much otherwise the chamfer will cut back past the *tsukeko*, leaving an unsightly gap.

Photograph 116 Take care with the top rail chamfer

Lightly chamfer all other edges of the top rail with your normal plane.

Finally, lightly chamfer all edges of the hip-board. The shoji is now ready to assemble.

Assembling the shoji

The *kasumi* kumiko do not extend the entire width, so extra care is needed in assembling the shoji. All mortises and tenons are glued as was done in the first shoji, but make sure no glue is attached to the hip-board or is squeezed out into the hip-board grooves.

First, attach the top and center rails to the kumiko panel. Insert this assembly into one of the stiles until the kumiko tenons start to enter their mortises in the stile, then insert the hip-board into its grooves. Insert the bottom rail into its mortises, and tap in.

Now attach the other stile, carefully tapping down with the *gennō* and hardwood block until the tenons enter their mortises. Once the tenons have become engaged, tap the stiles with slightly more force. Finally, clamp where the rails meet the stiles so that the joints are fully engaged. If necessary, you can clamp across the kumiko panel, but only where the horizontal kumiko join the stiles, and only apply fairly light clamping pressure. Also, make sure the shoji is square as you clamp.

Once the glue has dried remove the clamps and inspect all joints, and check for square.

Mark the location of the door pulls on the stiles as shown in Diagram 83 on Page 103 and cut out the housing mortise. Be careful not to mar the face of the shoji. This step can be done before applying water to raise the grain if you prefer, but the pull should not be inserted at that time.

Attaching the paper

Attach the paper in exactly the same way as described for the first shoji (see from Page 94).

Fitting and adjusting the shoji

This final procedure is generally the same as described in the first shoji (see from Page 95). The only substantial difference is in cutting the rebate for the top.

Once the bottom has been properly adjusted, put the shoji back on the front ledge of the bottom track and place the top against the top track as was explained for the first shoji. Make a light pencil mark on the back of the each of the stiles where they meet the track. This is the top rebate shoulder mark. Measure up about 14 mm and cut off the horns at those second marks.

Place a mark about 21 mm from the back of the stile, and cut down along this line until the rebate shoulder mark. Cut across this shoulder mark to make the rebate (see Diagram 84 on Page 104). When making this cut, take care not to overcut and cut into or mark the front face of the rail.

Any final minor adjustments to fit can now be made with the *kiwa-ganna* or shoulder plane.

Photograph 117 Project completed

This shoji has given you a number of options beyond the standard *aragumi mizugoshi-shōji*. The *kasumi-gumi* is a very attractive pattern that lends itself to many variations which can add tremendous interest to a room. The hip-board gives added stability to the shoji, and while traditionally, there are set sizes for the hip-board based on old paper sizes and the old measuring system, these constraints can be safely ignored provided the shoji maintains a sense of balance. Finally, although it doesn't convey the same feeling of quality that the *maru-zan* does, the *nageshi-zan* style of top rail certainly has its own charm, and provides you with additional joinery options.

MAKING A *KAWARI-GUMI* SHOJI

Photograph 118 *Kawari-gumi mizugoshi-shōji* **with** *izutsu-tsunagi* **base**

In this section I'll describe how to make a *kawari-gumi* shoji with the *mizugoshi* structure, and the *izutsu-tsunagi* kumiko pattern. The term *kawari* in regards to shoji simply means a variation, so essentially any pattern that varies from the traditional form is called a *kawari-gumi*. It is also often used when the internal kumiko alternate between left and right.

Although quite simple, this pattern is challenging, as all miters must join with just the right amount of tension, otherwise the pattern can look very untidy. There is a way of doing this, and I'll explain this as I go through the cutting and fitting process.

As with the previous *kasumi-gumi* shoji, the two panels are a mirror image of each other, so care must be taken when cutting the joints and the mortises.

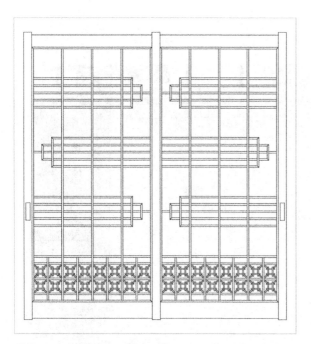

Diagram 102 The two panels are a mirror image

The kumiko pattern that forms the base for this shoji is one of the many that fall under the term *izutsu-tsunagi*, and is explained in detail in the relevant section.

The other patterns I describe in this book can also be used here, especially the *asa-no-ha*.

Although very time-consuming, these patterns are indeed the fun part of shoji and kumiko design, and how you incorporate them will give your shoji a completely unique feel that can be as subtle or as unrestrained as you like.

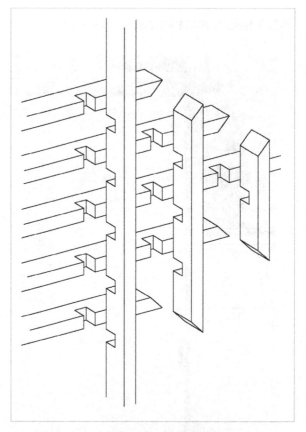

Diagram 103 Kumiko joinery details

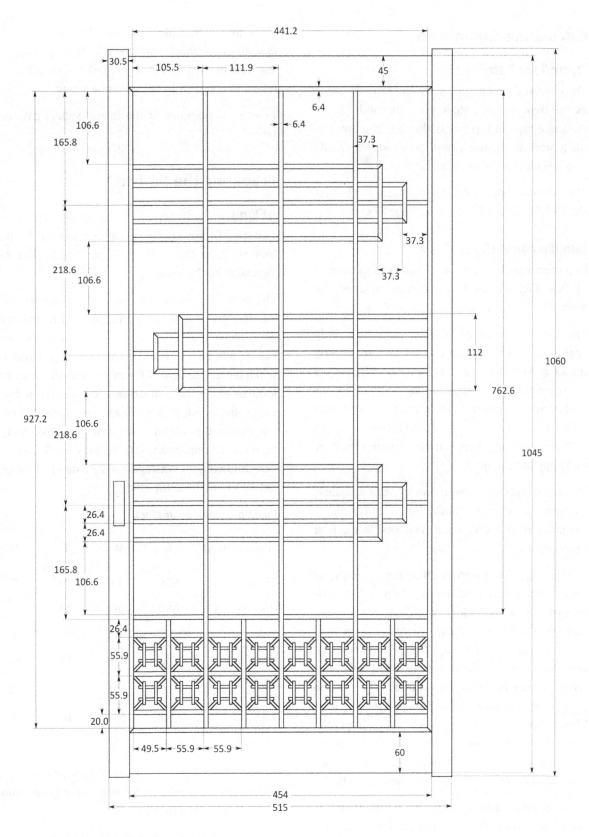

Diagram 104 Shoji dimension details

Calculating dimensions

Overall shoji size

The overall shoji dimensions are exactly the same as the two previous shoji. For this shoji, I'll use the same type of top rail as the first shoji (*maru-zan*), and the joinery will also be the same (*jaguchi* joint on both top and bottom rails).

The internal space is exactly the same as the first shoji — 441.2 x 927.2 mm (see Page 77).

Kumiko calculations

In patterns such as this, there is a certain amount of flexibility on kumiko intervals to alter the overall feel of the shoji.

The three vertical kumiko have to be evenly spaced so these intervals are set, and are exactly the same as in the first shoji (see Page 78), but we can vary the horizontal kumiko intervals to our preference. I decided to give the horizontal kumiko an interval of 20 mm, which gives sufficient spacing between the kumiko so they don't appear cramped.

The *izutsu-tsunagi* pattern has to fit in a square, so there's no choice with the bottom intervals — the pitch is 55.9 x 55.9 mm (rounded to the first decimal).

Calculating the intervals between groups of horizontal kumiko is also quite simple — consider each group as a single entity. There are five kumiko of 6.4 mm, and four spaces of 20 mm, so each group is 112 mm. The internal space between the top *tsukeko* and the top of the upper base kumiko is 762.6 mm, and there are three groups of 112 mm, so 762.6 – 336 = 426.6 mm. There are three groups so four intervals: 426.6 ÷ 4 = 106.65 mm. Therefore the interval between groups is 106.6 mm (there is a small amount of accuracy leeway with this interval).

On a kumiko pattern design point, contrast this with the calculations for the previous *kasumi-gumi* shoji. In this shoji the upper groups and the bottom pattern group are clearly divided by a single horizontal kumiko extending the entire width, so we can safely space the upper groups at even intervals. This was not the case for the *kasumi-gumi* shoji, and the V-shape opening at the bottom had to be accounted for visually, so trial and error for balance was necessary.

I cover calculations for the *izutsu-tsunagi* pattern later.

Preparing the timber

Milling

The shoji frame will be exactly the same as in the first shoji, so the rail, stile and *tsukeko* dimensions will be the same.

The ends of some of the vertical and horizontal kumiko are joined with miters, so the *mikomi* measurement of both will be the same. In this case it will be 15 mm. The *izutsu-tsunagi* kumiko will have a *mitsuke* of 4.0 mm because the thinner kumiko make the pattern feel less cluttered and more balanced. Since there are many short kumiko in this pattern, working out how many kumiko are required is largely guesswork. In this case, allowing for wastage, the 15 listed in Table 4 below should be sufficient.

Cutting List (in millimeters)

Component	L	W	T	N
Top rail	550	45	29	2
Bottom rail	550	60	29	2
Stile	1,110	30.5	30.5	4
Kumiko	1,100	6.4	15	35
Pattern kumiko	1,100	4.0	15	15
Tsukeko	1,100	6.4	16	6
Story stick	1,300	20	20	1

L: Length (cut oversize); W: Width (*mitsuke*); T: Thickness (*mikomi*); N: Number (this is the minimum number required)

Table 4 *Kawari-gumi* **shoji cutting list**

Marking

The marking process is exactly the same as in the other shoji. Points to note here are that the four short vertical kumiko at the bottom are fitted after the *tsukeko* have been attached, so the ends are cut slightly oversize, then trimmed to fit. They do not have tenons, so do not cut mortises in the *tsukeko* and bottom rail for these pieces.

Story stick

Mark the story stick with all stile, rail and kumiko markings with a sharp marking knife.

For the three upper groups, mark the main horizontal kumiko first, then the shorter kumiko measured from the main kumiko in their respective groups.

Similar to the *kasumi-gumi* shoji, most of the horizontal kumiko do not extend all the way across, and these should be clearly marked on the story stick. The joint locations for the short vertical kumiko that close off the horizontal kumiko should also be clearly indicated.

Stiles

Mark the mortise locations on all stiles as shown in the following diagrams. There is no need for a *tsukeko* mortise in the bottom of the stiles, but because of the wide interval at the top, the *tsukeko* there will need to be joined as in the first shoji, so a *tsukeko* mortise is required at the top of the stiles.

Pay particular attention to the location of the mortises for the horizontal kumiko, and which kumiko extend to the stiles, and which do not.

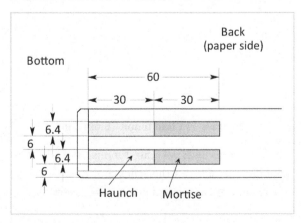

Diagram 105 Stile mortises — bottom

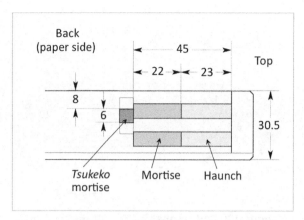

Diagram 106 Stile mortises – top

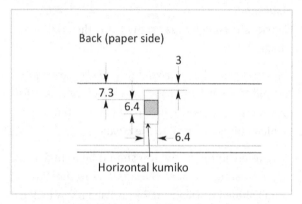

Diagram 107 Stile mortises – kumiko

Rails

The rails are exactly the same as in the first shoji, so mark the tenons and mortise locations as shown in the following diagrams.

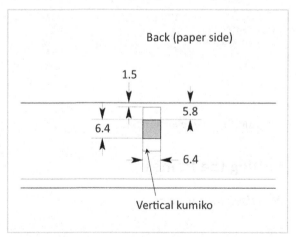

Diagram 108 Rail mortises – kumiko

121

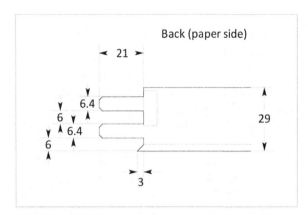

Diagram 109 Rail tenons

Tsukeko

Mark all *tsukeko* as shown in the following diagram.

Mortises in the horizontal *tsukeko* are quite straightforward, but as in the case of the stiles, for the vertical *tsukeko* pay particular attention to which kumiko extend to the *tsukeko*.

The miter joints at the top should be joined as in the first shoji, so mark these miters to the dimensions shown in Diagram 74 on Page 83. A tack or small nail will suffice for the miter joints at the bottom, as was done in the *kasumi-gumi* shoji.

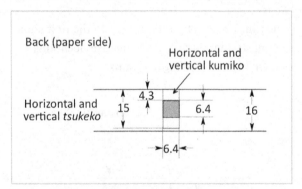

Diagram 110 *Tsukeko* mortises

Cutting the frames

Mortises and tenons

Stiles

First, check again that the mortises for the kumiko are marked in their correct position.

Cut out the mortises for the rail tenons, *tsukeko* and kumiko in the stiles using your preferred method. The mortises for the rail tenons are

22 mm deep, and the haunch housing is a fraction deeper than 8 mm. The mortises for the *tsukeko* are 5.5 mm deep. The mortises for the kumiko are 7.5 mm deep. There is a 1.5 mm offset between the backs of the stiles and the rails, and also between the backs of the rails and *tsukeko*, so take extra care with the position of the mortises in relation to the back.

Rails

Cut the mortises for the kumiko to a depth of 7.5 mm.

Cut the *jaguchi* on the rails as explained in the exercise from Page 72, then cut the tenons and trim the haunches to the dimensions shown in the following diagram.

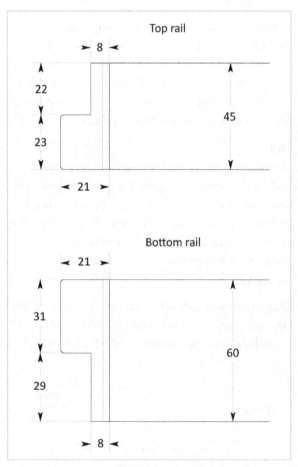

Diagram 111 Rail tenon dimensions

Chamfer the ends of the tenons, but do not chamfer the sides of the stiles and rails — these are chamfered at the end just before assembly.

Tsukeko

Cut the mortises in the *tsukeko*. These are through mortises, so make sure the back face where the mortise came through is clean of waste.

Cut the end miter joints at the top as shown in Diagram 74 on Page 83 and as explained in the first shoji (Pages 86 and 87). Chamfer the front inner edges of all *tsukeko*.

Rebates

Cut the rebates in the rails as shown in the following diagram and as explained in the first shoji (Page 88).

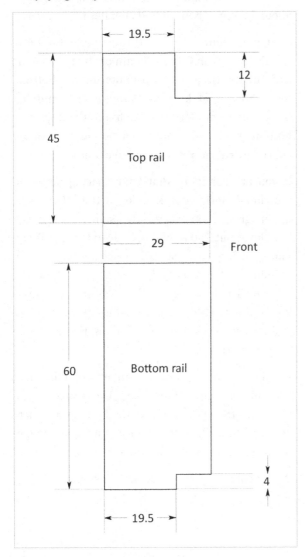

Diagram 112 Rebate dimension detail

Raising the grain

Place the *tsukeko* safely to one side. Thoroughly wet a piece of cloth and wipe the water liberally over the rails and stiles, then place to one side and allow to dry.

Cutting and assembling the kumiko

Unlike the previous two shoji, the *mikomi* of the vertical and horizontal kumiko is the same at 15 mm.

Mark the backs of the kumiko with pencil marks, but do not chamfer the fronts. The grain on the front of the kumiko for the *kawari-gumi* pattern should be as straight as possible, so examine the kumiko and select the fronts carefully.

Similar to the previous *kasumi-gumi* shoji, this shoji presents a challenge when cutting the kumiko because not all horizontal kumiko extend all the way across. To reduce the possibility of error when cutting the horizontal kumiko, I use the following kumiko and joint numbering system for this shoji.

This numbering system is only a suggestion, and it works for me; if you prefer a different way, then by all means use that, as long as you understand it and it works.

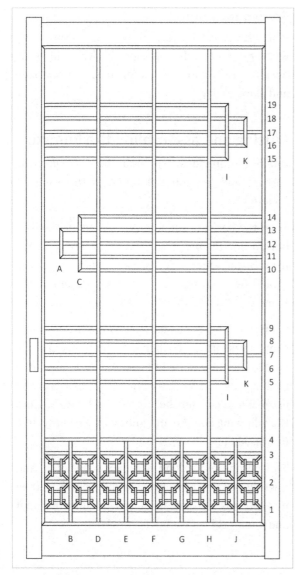

Diagram 113 Suggested numbering system – left shoji

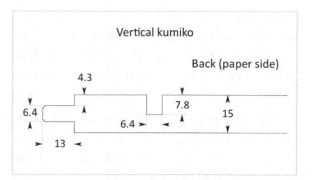

Diagram 114 Vertical kumiko joinery

Vertical kumiko

Provided you take sufficient care the cutting sequence for the vertical kumiko does not really matter, but this is the way I tackle it. All cuts for the vertical kumiko are made on the back.

Secure the six long vertical kumiko for both shoji panels (D, F and H) in the kumiko cutting jig and cut the 19 half-lap joints for all horizontal kumiko. The half-lap joints should be cut to a depth of about 7.8 mm. Then cut and chamfer the tenons.

Next, cut eight short vertical kumiko for both panels (B, E, G and J) to a length of about 200 mm, and cut the three half-lap joints for the bottom three horizontal kumiko (kumiko 1, 2 and 3). Make sure you leave enough on the top and bottom so you can trim to size. Remember, these short vertical kumiko do not have tenons.

If you are confident that your spacing between individual horizontal kumiko within the three upper groups is exactly the same, secure six kumiko about 200 mm long and cut three half-lap joints, using any of the relevant horizontal kumiko markings — 6, 7, 8; or 11, 12, 13; or 16, 17, 18. These pieces will close off the outer horizontal kumiko in each group (C and I), so make sure you leave enough on the top and bottom for the 45° miter.

Finally, secure six kumiko about 100 mm long and cut a single half-lap joint. These pieces will close off the inner horizontal kumiko in each group (A and K), so make sure you leave enough on the top and bottom for the 45° miter.

Do not cut any of the miters at this stage.

Horizontal kumiko

Cutting the horizontal kumiko can become somewhat confusing, so work carefully to the plan as you make your cuts.

All cuts for the horizontal kumiko are made on the front.

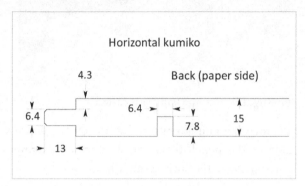

Diagram 115 Horizontal kumiko joinery

This is the sequence I use for the left-hand shoji. The right-hand shoji is a mirror image of the left, so you will have to keep this in mind when making the cuts for it.

The kumiko cutting jig is not wide enough to hold all 19 kumiko, which in any event would be too difficult to manage, so you will need to split this in two. Secure the kumiko in the jig front up and cut the joints for the three long vertical kumiko (joints D, F and H). Then cut the left and right tenons. Do not cut off the ends of the tenons at this stage. Some of these tenons will be discarded, but cutting them together is more efficient.

Secure the bottom three kumiko (kumiko 1, 2 and 3) and cut joints B, E, G and J. This set of four cuts is the same for both panels, so you can combine the kumiko for the two panels. Remove the kumiko once these cuts have been made.

It is also possible and much quicker to join kumiko from both panels for the next cuts, but you must be very careful and make sure you observe the plan closely and cut the correct kumiko in the correct position if you decide to proceed in this way. I will, however, only describe the sequence for cutting the left-hand shoji.

Secure kumiko 11, 12 and 13 in the jig and cut joint C. Remove kumiko 11 and 13, and cut kumiko 12 at joint A.

Next, secure kumiko 6, 7, 8, 16, 17 and 18 in the jig and cut joint I. Remove kumiko 6, 8, 16 and 18 and cut kumiko 7 and 17 at joint K.

The cuts for the right-hand shoji are the same, except the cuts A and C, and I and K are reversed.

Cut off the ends of the tenons and chamfer. That completes the kumiko cutting.

Assembling

First assemble the full-length vertical and horizontal kumiko, ensuring you have the correct left/right and top/bottom orientation.

Photograph 119 Assemble full-length kumiko first

Next is the most difficult aspect of this pattern — cutting the miters joining the shorter vertical and horizontal kumiko.

The miter joint is held together with a dab of glue and just the right amount of tension. If the tension is too great or not enough, or if one side is too long or too short, the miter will open up or will be lop-sided, so care must be taken with every miter.

The following is the method I use, and while it can be slightly time-consuming, I've found it is the best way to achieve good consistent results.

It is very easy to make errors in miter orientation, so the easiest way to avoid this is to align the pairs of kumiko and place a rough orientation mark well past the cut-off length, as shown in the following photograph.

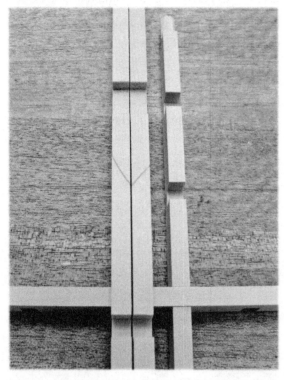

Photograph 120 Rough miter orientation marks to prevent errors

The horizontal kumiko are always inserted first, followed by the short vertical kumiko. When inserting the horizontal kumiko, it makes no difference whether you start with the inner or outer pairs of the three groups. For the sake of the exercise, I started with the inner pairs (horizontal kumiko 6 and 8; 11 and 13; and 16 and 18).

Rest each kumiko upside-down next to its adjacent kumiko that has already been assembled so that the half-lap joint is partially engaged, and place a pencil mark at the joint where the miter is to be cut, as shown in the following photograph.

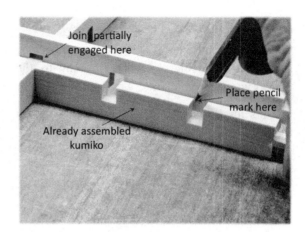

Photograph 121 Mark miter location

Remove the kumiko and cut at 45° on the waste side of the pencil mark you just made, making sure you have the correct miter orientation.

Using the 45° shooting board or the 45° jig, whichever you prefer, trim the 45° miter to the point where the inside edge of the miter is slightly longer than its half-lap position — this should be no more than the thickness of one or two shavings, as shown in the following photograph. Work carefully here, and regularly check to make sure you don't trim off too much.

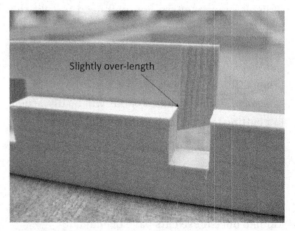

Photograph 122 Trim the miter joint

Repeat for all inner pairs, and glue into place. Do not trim the short vertical kumiko at this stage.

Photograph 123 Assemble inner pairs

Next, go through exactly the same procedure for the outer pairs (kumiko 5 and 9; 10 and 14; and 15 and 19), and glue into place.

Photograph 124 Repeat for outer pairs and assemble

The next step is to trim the longer of the short vertical kumiko (kumiko C and I). The process is essentially the same, though you now have to trim both ends.

Photograph 125 Trim the longer kumiko first

As in the case of the horizontal kumiko, the miters for these vertical kumiko should be trimmed slightly over-length, but no more than the thickness of one or two shavings. Once they have been trimmed, glue them into place.

Photograph 126 Assemble the longer kumiko

When the longer of the short vertical kumiko have been assembled, trim the shorter of the short vertical kumiko (kumiko A and K), following exactly the same procedure, and assemble. This sequence of assembling the longer vertical kumiko before the shorter kumiko is important. Do not assemble the shorter kumiko before the longer kumiko are in place.

Photograph 127 Trim and assemble shorter kumiko

If you have followed this process and trimmed the miters carefully so they are just over-length, the miter joints should be tight-fitting with no gaps.

If you look closely at the miters, you will notice that the ends of the kumiko are pushed out very slightly. In the following photograph, I've placed a straightedge firmly against the miter section of the kumiko, and you can detect the smallest of gaps at the half-lap joint. This indicates a slight amount of tension on the miter joint, and is exactly what you should aim for.

Photograph 128 Correct amount of tension on miter

Next attach the *tsukeko*, making sure that the kumiko tenons are firmly engaged in their respective mortises in the *tsukeko*, especially the bottom three horizontal kumiko. The top miter joints are held together by the mortises and tenons, while thin tacks or nails through the miters from the stile side will suffice for the bottom miters. After attaching the *tsukeko*, set the assembled frame aside to allow the glue to dry thoroughly.

Once the glue has dried, trim the bottom short vertical kumiko (kumiko B, E, G and J) at both ends to fit. I use a 90° shooting board, which is exactly the same as my 45° shooting board, except the fence is set at 90° instead of 45°.

Trim carefully, because too much tension at the bottom could force open gaps between the major vertical kumiko and the *tsukeko*. However, gaps will also appear if there is not enough tension. Here, too, the difference between too much and

not enough is the thickness of one or two plane shavings. When trimmed, apply glue to the half-lap joints and the two ends, and insert.

Photograph 129 Trim the bottom carefully

Repeat for all kumiko, then set aside to allow the glue to dry thoroughly. Follow the same procedure for the right-hand shoji, but remember that it is a mirror image of the left-hand shoji.

Photograph 130 Completed kumiko pattern

Once the glue has dried, it's on to the *izutsu-tsunagi* pattern, and the fun part begins.

Izutsu-tsunagi pattern

Izutsu is the Japanese term for well curb, the parallel crossed supporting structure around a well, and this pattern has been used in motifs, designs and also literature since ancient times. *Tsunagi* simply means "join" or "connect". There are quite a few different kinds of *izutsu-tsunagi* patterns with various ways of securing the central square cross shape. The one we tackle here is probably the simplest of those patterns, but the uncluttered feel makes it look quite stunning in a row across the width of a shoji or bordering another pattern.

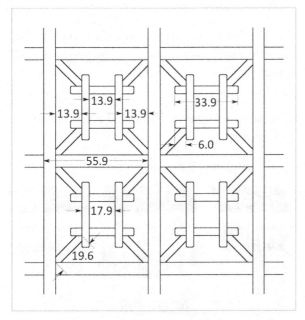

Diagram 116 *Izutsu-tsunagi* dimension details

As can be seen in the diagram above, it consists of a square held in place by four diagonal locking pieces extending from corner to corner. The balance between the square framing structure (called *jigumi* when it forms the base for intricate kumiko patterns) and the internal square is critical, and in this case, I've opted for even intervals between the components of the square and the *jigumi* kumiko (the intervals are slightly out because of rounding). The measurement for the interval is calculated in the same way as when calculating normal kumiko intervals.

A slight chamfer on the top and side edges of the ends of the square gives the pattern a sense of polish. The locking pieces are trimmed to fit using the 45° jig (Diagram 82 Page 102).

The internal kumiko have a *mitsuke* of 4.0 mm to prevent a cluttered feel within the pattern. The pitch of the internal square is 17.9 mm, and the ends of the kumiko extend past the joint by 6.0 mm. The locking pieces are 19.6 mm, but in practice, their length can vary slightly, so they are trimmed to fit.

First, make up 32 squares for the two shoji panels. For this, simply group a comfortable number of kumiko in the kumiko cutting jig — say eight or twelve — and cut the half-lap joints in pairs with a pitch of 17.9 mm. Make sure you leave enough on either side of the joint pairs for the 6 mm extension.

Cut away the first group of joint pairs, and flip half over so that the joints are facing up in half and down in the other half. The kumiko with the joints facing up will be the horizontal kumiko, and those with the joints facing down will be the vertical kumiko.

Trim the ends to a 6 mm extension, and chamfer the tops and side of the ends with the 45° jig as was done for the *kasumi* kumiko in the previous shoji (see Pages 112 and 113).

Assemble the squares, making sure the chamfers on the vertical and horizontal kumiko are facing upward.

Repeat this process until you have made up the required 32 squares.

Place one square inside one of the *jigumi* squares, making sure that the horizontal and vertical kumiko are oriented correctly (the vertical kumiko is on top of the horizontal kumiko).

Photograph 131 Ensure the correct horizontal / vertical kumiko orientation

Trim a locking piece to about 19.6 mm on the 45° jig. Holding and trimming the short pieces in the jig may feel awkward at first, but it becomes much easier and faster with practice. Make sure that the vertex of the 90° angle at the end is exactly in the center.

Photograph 132 Trim first locking piece to size

Glue this locking piece to the corners of the internal square and *jigumi* square. Trim the diagonally opposite locking piece to size and insert in the corners to hold the square in place. This should be a firm fit, but it should not be forced.

Photograph 133 Insert diagonal locking pieces to hold the square

Repeat this for the other two locking pieces. The final locking piece is the critical piece, and it should be firm enough to lock the square securely in place.

A small dab of glue can be added to the corners if you prefer.

Photograph 134 The final locking piece is the key

This completes one square.

Photograph 135 First square completed

After completing all *jigumi* squares on one shoji panel, repeat for the second shoji.

Photograph 136 Continue inserting squares

Take extra care when inserting the squares at the ends next to the *tsukeko*, because if the fit is too tight or the locking pieces are forced in, there is a risk that the *tsukeko* will be pushed away from the kumiko and a gap will open up. A slightly easier fit with glue attached to all corners and both ends of the locking pieces will prevent this.

Photograph 137 First panel completed

Planing the rails and stiles

The shoji frame is exactly the same as the frame in the first shoji, so the processes detailed for that shoji apply here as well (see Page 93).

Assembling the shoji

Similarly, the processes detailed in assembling the first shoji also apply to this shoji (see Page 93).

However, care must be taken when tapping the stiles into the rail tenons. If the stiles are hit with too much force by the *gennō* and hardwood block, there is a high risk that the kumiko miter joints may be jarred loose, especially if the joints do not have sufficient tension. To prevent this from happening, tap carefully, and if necessary, bring the mortise and tenon joints together with clamps.

When the shoji have dried thoroughly, inspect the join between the *jaguchi* and the chamfers in the top and bottom rails, and plane flush with the stile if required (see Photograph 83 on Page 94). This should only take a couple of very light shavings.

Mark the location for the door pulls in the stiles and cut out the housing mortise. I decided to place the door pulls level with the middle of the bottom group of shoji, but they could equally have been located centrally between the bottom and middle groups of shoji. The location is entirely your own preference.

When cutting the housing mortise, be careful not to mar the face of the shoji. This step can be done before applying water to raise the grain if you prefer, but the pull should not be inserted at that time.

Attaching the paper

Attach the paper in exactly the same way as described for the first shoji (see Page 94). There are many more kumiko to which glue has to be applied, so you will need to work efficiently to ensure that the glue doesn't dry before you're ready to attach the paper.

Fitting and adjusting the shoji

This final procedure is exactly the same as detailed for the first shoji (see from Page 95).

Photograph 138 Project completed

This is quite a challenging shoji to make, but with care and accuracy in marking and cutting, it will come together very well. The patterns in this shoji are the launching pad for a vast array of attractive and complex designs — the *kawari-gumi* for the beautiful *kōzu* patterns, and the *izutsu-tsunagi* for the many other more intricate *izutsu* patterns.

A faster way of cutting pattern kumiko — *Ha-ganna*

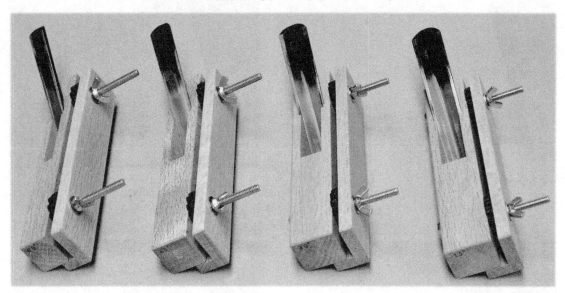

Ha-ganna are highly specialized planes used only in kumiko work. They were developed many years ago by the Japanese Tategu Craft Association (Tategu Kōgei Kenkyū-Kai) to speed up the process of cutting the small pieces for the various kumiko patterns, and without them, the very minute and highly elaborate patterns would be extremely difficult and far too time-consuming, and therefore cost-prohibitive.

There are four planes in this group and they are designed to cut at 60°, 45°, 30°, and 15°. The plane I used for the *izutsu-tsunagi* was the 45° plane, and the following describes how it's used. Of course, all of the patterns I detail in this book and in subsequent books can be made without the use of these planes.

The blade is projected to cut just over half the kumiko thickness. A manageable number of kumiko are held on a jig.

The plane is drawn across the kumiko to cut a 90° V-groove.

133

The kumiko are flipped over...

And the plane is drawn across to cut a 90° V-groove on the back.

The kumiko are separated at the groove...

To leave locking pieces with clean 90° angle ends.

These planes have an adjustable fence so the lengths of the pieces cut off are generally the same. Any minor difference in length covers minor differences in the sizes of the *jigumi* squares created by the base kumiko. Therefore a locking piece of exactly the correct length is always readily available.

Estimates by a number of *tategu* associations have credited these planes with up to a ten-fold increase in speed of cutting pattern kumiko.

Kumiko patterns

Photograph 139 Partitioning screen (*tsuitate*) dating back to the early 1800s with a simple but effective kumiko pattern

In this section I'll describe how to make two additional kumiko patterns — the *futae kaku-tsunagi*, and the *asa-no-ha*.

These patterns require no new skills other than those acquired making the three shoji in this book, and the only new jigs required are for the *asa-no-ha*.

The patterns will be made into kumiko frames, rather than complete shoji, but the descriptions and explanations will enable you to apply these patterns to your own shoji.

Some of the joinery is quite challenging, so be patient and accurate, and enjoy this truly fascinating side of shoji design.

Futae kaku-tsunagi

Photograph 140 *Futae kaku-tsunagi* pattern

If you look closely, you can see that the *futae kaku-tsunagi* is connected to the *kawari-gumi* pattern in the previous shoji. The pattern also strengthens the skill foundations for making the much more complex *kōzu* patterns. *Futae* means "double", and *kaku* in this case means a "90° angle". As I mentioned before, *tsunagi* means "join" or "connect".

The pattern itself can be applied in a similar way to the *kawari-gumi* pattern in which it forms a large feature, or it can be reduced in size to form an attractive band or border. The use of different colored timber within the pattern can also add further interest.

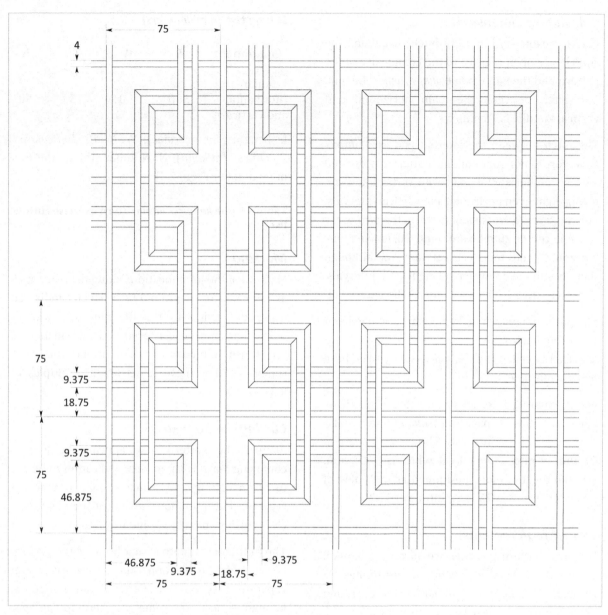

Diagram 117 Detailed dimensions of the *futae kaku-tsunagi* pattern

Calculating dimensions

For this exercise, I chose a pitch that would be sufficiently open relative to the complexity of the pattern and the kumiko *mitsuke*, which is 4.0 mm. The pitch between the main horizontal and vertical kumiko is 75 mm.

The pitch between the internal pattern kumiko, however, is not random. Each square is divided with seven horizontal and seven vertical kumiko, giving eight even horizontal and vertical intervals. For the *futae kaku-tsunagi* pattern, the two outer and one center kumiko are removed, leaving four horizontal and four vertical kumiko, although there is still the equivalent of eight even intervals. This gives the pattern its wonderful balanced feel.

The pattern in which no kumiko are removed and all seven horizontal and seven vertical kumiko are used is called the *yae kaku-tsunagi. Yae* here means "multiple".

For calculating internal pitch: pitch = width or height of internal space + *mitsuke* of one kumiko ÷ number of even intervals. The internal space is 71 mm, so pitch = 71 + 4 ÷ 8, which is 9.375 mm. Kumiko are therefore positioned at multiples of this pitch; e.g., 46.875 is a multiple of 9.375.

Timber requirements

For these pattern exercises, we only need kumiko, so there's no requirement to prepare timber for rails, stiles, *tsukeko* or hip-boards. Moreover, one of the kumiko can be used as a story stick.

Cutting List (in millimeters)

Component	L	W	T	N
Kumiko (horizontal and vertical)	500	4.0	15	50
L: Length (cut oversize); W: Width (*mitsuke*); T: Thickness (*mikomi*); N: Number (this is the minimum number required)				

Table 5 *Futae kaku-tsunagi* **pattern exercise cutting list**

Marking

Mark all of the joint locations along the story stick as indicated in Diagram 117. I haven't indicated every dimension in the diagram otherwise it would become too cluttered and unreadable, so for those dimensions that aren't indicated, remember that these joints are in multiples of 9.375 mm.

Cutting the kumiko

At first the pattern may appear like a very confusing maze with no clear indication of where to begin cutting and which kumiko can be cut together, but if you look closely at the diagram, a clear cutting strategy should begin to emerge.

The first point to note is that because the pattern is symmetrical, we don't have to worry about separate cuts for the vertical and horizontal kumiko — make the same cut, then flip half over so the joint is facing down, and these are the vertical kumiko.

As strange as it may seem with a pattern of this apparent complexity, there are in fact only two different groups of cuts. These I've shown with asterisks and dashes in the following diagram.

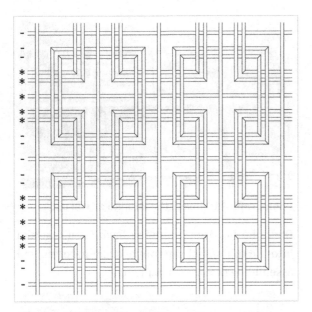

Diagram 118 Kumiko cutting groups

As you can see, one group has ten kumiko, and the other has eleven. Cut each group twice, and that covers all 42 horizontal and vertical kumiko.

Photograph 141 shows the story stick I used with color-coded marks for the cuts. Unfortunately this doesn't show up in the black and white photograph, so I've indicated the three colors — red, blue and green. I used red for the *jigumi* joints, and these are common cuts for both groups. I used blue to indicate the cuts shown with the asterisk in the diagram above, and green for the cuts shown with a dash. This removes any possibility of making the wrong cut in the wrong kumiko.

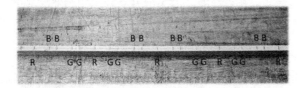

Photograph 141 Story stick showing color-coded cutting marks

Transfer the appropriate marks from the story stick to each of the four groups for cutting, but do not cut the story stick.

Although some of the joints you cut will be discarded as you trim the miters for the internal squares, this is by far the most efficient way of cutting this pattern.

The kumiko *mikomi* is 15 mm, so cut the half-lap joints to a depth of about 7.8 mm.

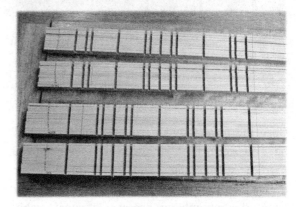

Photograph 142 Kumiko in their respective groups

Photograph 142 shows the cut kumiko separated into their respective groups. The top two groups are the "asterisk" kumiko (one group is the vertical kumiko and the other group is the horizontal kumiko), and the bottom two groups are the "dash" kumiko. You can also clearly see the common cuts for the *jigumi* joints. I also cut a couple of spares in case disaster strikes and I snap a kumiko.

Assembling the pattern

As with most patterns, the main vertical and horizontal kumiko should be assembled first. These form the *jigumi* squares into which the pattern kumiko are inserted.

Be very careful when assembling the kumiko because the pieces between pairs of cuts are just over 5 mm and therefore very weak, so they can easily break off if the kumiko are handled roughly.

139

Photograph 143 Assemble main kumiko first

Once the main kumiko are assembled, we then have to work out a strategy for assembling the pattern kumiko. Since there are many more miters in this pattern than in the *kawari-gumi* shoji, the assembling process is considerably more difficult.

There is no established sequence, but I've found that the easiest way is to assemble the horizontal kumiko first (joints facing upward), then insert the vertical kumiko.

Whatever sequence you decide to adopt, the mitering process is exactly the same as in the *kawari-gumi* shoji.

Photograph 144 Mark miter location

Rest each horizontal kumiko upside-down next to the adjacent main horizontal kumiko so that the half-lap joint is partially engaged, and place a pencil mark at the joint where the miter is to be cut, as shown in Photograph 144.

Insert the kumiko into the frame as you cut them.

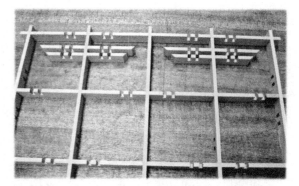

Photograph 145 Insert the kumiko as you cut

Once the horizontal kumiko have been inserted into the top half of the frame, begin mitering and assembling the vertical kumiko.

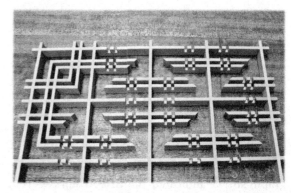

Photograph 146 Assemble horizontal kumiko before vertical kumiko

Once the top half has been completed, begin inserting the horizontal kumiko in the bottom half (Photograph 147).

Photograph 147 Continue on to the bottom half

Continue assembling the horizontal then vertical kumiko. In this kind of pattern the kumiko are all interconnected, and the tension applied to the miter joints to obtain a tight join is transmitted to all the adjacent kumiko, so toward the end the joints may not come together as easily as they did at the start. Therefore, as you reach the end, take extra care when inserting the kumiko and do not force them in.

Photograph 148 Toward the end take extra care when inserting the final few kumiko

This stunning pattern is quite a challenge to make, and it requires full concentration to ensure the joints fit and the miters are facing the correct way. Accuracy, though, is the key, so work carefully without trying to rush through, and you'll enjoy the wonderful sense of achievement as the final kumiko slides in.

Photograph 149 Completed pattern

Asa-no-ha

Photograph 150 There are four different methods of cutting the *asa-no-ha* pattern

The *asa-no-ha* (hemp leaf) is perhaps the quintessential floral pattern in the square *jigumi* structure and also in the much more complex diamond *jigumi*. Its simple and ancient design has remained popular down through the centuries. The hemp plant grows quickly and straight, so in the past the pattern has often been used in children's clothing to encourage their healthy growth. In Japan it has been used in weaving, dyeing, traditional paper manufacture, and, of course, in woodworking, particularly in kumiko art and craft.

In the square *asa-no-ha*, four squares combine to form one pattern. Pieces trimmed at 45° on both sides to form a 90° point at both ends are inserted from the center of the squares to the corners. This splits the four squares into eight triangles, and we now have our base on which to work.

There are four ways of cutting the hinge: *genkotsu* (two methods), *ori-mage*, and *jaguchi*. The small locking pieces vary for each of these methods. All four ways require slightly different jigs, and I'll describe them in their respective sections. There are two jigs common to all. These are the 45° jig shown at Diagram 82 on Page 102, and a 22.5° jig, which is exactly the same as the 45° jig, except the angle is 22.5° instead of 45°, as shown in the following diagram. You can make separate jigs, or you can make one end 45° and the other end 22.5°, as I have done.

In this book I only describe the square *asa-no-ha*. The geometry and characteristics of the *asa-no-ha* in the diamond *jigumi* are completely different, so the difficulties faced and the angles used in the *asa-no-ha* for the two are not the same.

In these explanations, I'll make one complete *asa-no-ha* for each method. In all examples the pitch is 50 mm, and the kumiko *mitsuke* is 4.0 mm. This is a good size for a drink coaster or a stand for a small vase.

Through this, I give you a range of options for cutting this wonderful pattern, but I would recommend that you choose the method you find easiest to use, and stay with that, rather than keep swapping among the different methods. You'll find that speed and accuracy will increase with practice, but only if you stick to the same method.

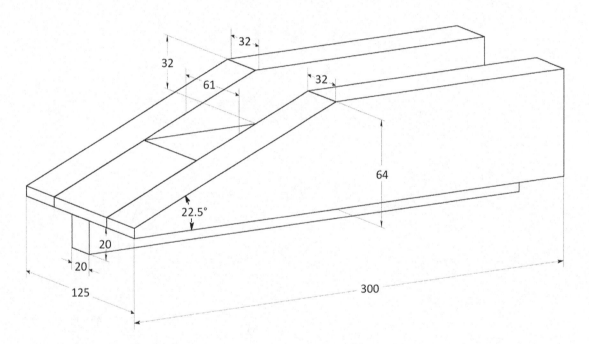

Diagram 119 22.5° jig

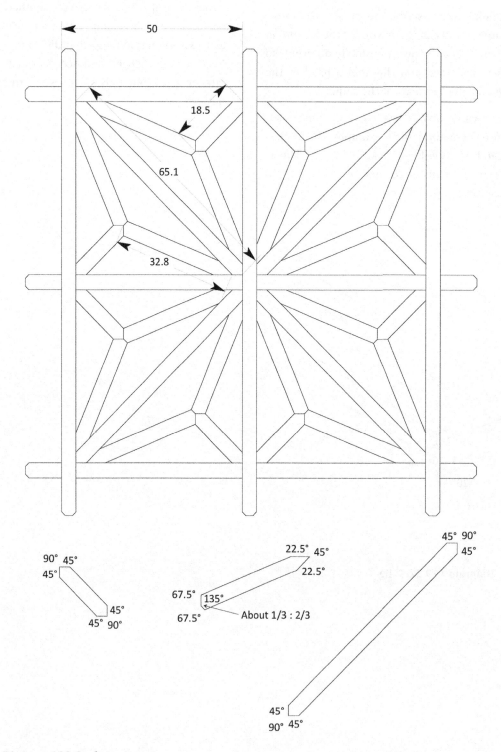

Diagram 120 *Genkotsu* type 1

The *genkotsu* method is one in which the hinge section consists of two separate pieces that are cut at set angles on either side to join and house the locking piece. This produces probably the weakest joint of the different methods, but provided the correct amount of tension is applied to the locking piece, the joint is sufficiently strong and will remain secure. Within this method you have a further two options — Type 1 and Type 2 — each requiring different jigs.

First, we'll look at Type 1.

Genkotsu Type 1 jig

The only additional jig you require for this method is one to cut the end angle at 67.5°. The jig I use for this is the same as the 45° and 22.5° jigs. An alternative jig is shown below.

There are two fences on the jig so there's the choice of using a Western plane or Japanese *kanna* to trim the pieces. Simply clamp this jig to the workbench, but you can attach a piece of wood on the bottom to secure the jig in the workbench vise if you prefer.

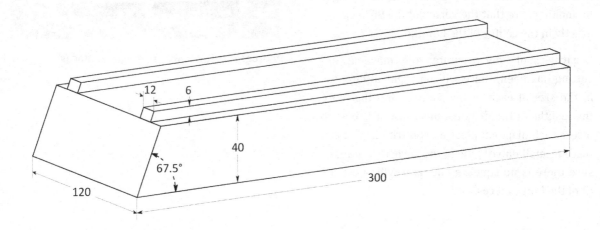

Diagram 121 67.5° jig

Base kumiko (jigumi)

The *jigumi* is very straightforward. Six kumiko with a 4.0 mm *mitsuke* and 15 mm *mikomi* are cut with a pitch of 50 mm, and assembled. Chamfer the ends on the sides and top, but do not chamfer the upper edges of the kumiko.

Photograph 152 Start with the diagonal pieces

Insert all four diagonal pieces, then move on to the hinge pieces.

Photograph 151 *Jigumi* with 50 mm pitch

Diagonal pieces

The first pieces to make up and insert are the four diagonal pieces. Cut these slightly over-length, and trim both ends on the 45° jig to about 65.1 mm. Trim the ends carefully to ensure a tight fit, making sure that the vertex of the 90° angle is exactly in the center of the kumiko.

Regardless of how accurate your marking and cutting has been, there will be slight differences in the size of each of the squares and therefore the lengths of the diagonal pieces, so it is best to insert each diagonal piece as you trim it. You can place a small dab of glue in the corners, but make sure there is no squeeze-out, as it will affect the fit of the hinge pieces.

Photograph 153 Insert all diagonal pieces

Hinge pieces

One end of the hinge piece forms a 45° point using the 22.5° jig, and the other end a 135° point using the 67.5° jig. You can start either end, but I find it easier to start at the 135° end.

Photograph 154 Trim ⅔:⅓ on the 67.5° jig

The vertex of this end is not in the center, but about ⅔ to one side. This is purely judgment, and the more *asa-no-ha* you make, the easier this judgment becomes. Once you are satisfied with the roughly ⅔:⅓ mix, begin trimming the other end.

Photograph 155 Trim the other end in the 22.5° jig

Trim the other end in the 22.5° jig to 32.8 mm, add a small dab of glue to the appropriate corners of the square, and insert the hinge pieces.

Photograph 156 Insert hinge pieces

Locking piece

The locking piece is the part that holds it all together. In this method the locking piece is very simple — both ends are trimmed to 90° points on the 45° jig.

The diagram shows a length of 18.5 mm, but this is really only a guide. You will need to trim the piece carefully until it forms a snug fit with the hinge pieces. This fit should be snug, but not excessively tight otherwise the frame will be distorted. Add a small dab of glue in the corner of the square, and in the hinge opening.

Photograph 157 Insert locking piece

Repeat this for all parts of the *jigumi*, and you have completed the *asa-no-ha*.

Photograph 158 Completed *asa-no-ha*

Summary

This method of cutting the *genkotsu* requires care and good judgment when trimming the hinge pieces where they join and house the locking piece, but provided your judgment is sound and the jigs are accurate, I believe this method gives the best and most consistent joints. This is my preferred method of making the square *asa-no-ha*.

Photograph 159 Type 1 hinges / locking piece relationship

Genkotsu — Type 2

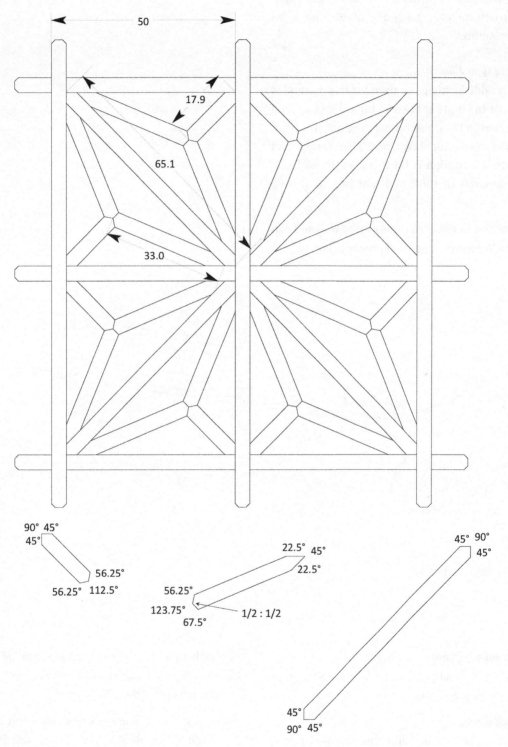

Diagram 122 *Genkotsu* type 2

This method of making the *genkotsu* is essentially the same as the first method, except some of the angles are slightly different. It has exactly the same structural advantages and disadvantages as the first method.

Genkotsu type 2 jig

The only additional jig required for this method is one to cut the ends at the 56° angle. I've included the fraction in the dimensional diagram (Diagram 122), but rounding down to 56° is more than adequate. The design is the same as the 67.5° jig in the previous method, and that jig will also be used.

I've attached two fences to this jig as well so I can use both Western planes and Japanese *kanna*.

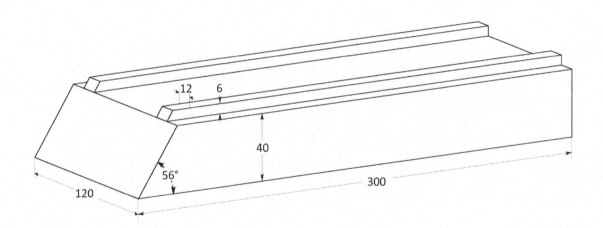

Diagram 123 56° jig

Base kumiko (jigumi)
The *jigumi* is exactly the same as the one used in the previous *asa-no-ha*.

Diagonal pieces
Since the *jigumi* is the same, the diagonal pieces are also the same as in the previous *asa-no-ha*.

Hinge pieces
One end of the hinge piece forms a 45° point using the 22.5° jig, and the other end close enough to a 123.5° point using the 67.5° jig and the 56° jig. You can start either end, but I find it easier to start at the 123.5° end.

The 123.5° end is made up of one angle at 67.5° and the other at 56°, and the vertex is in the center of the kumiko. Note that the 56° angle is on the outer side of the pattern and houses the locking piece. Trim the 67.5° side first, and place a pencil mark on the part you have just trimmed so you can quickly determine which way the piece faces when inserting.

Once you are satisfied with this end, trim the other end in the 22.5° jig to the required 33.0 mm. Add a small dab of glue to the appropriate corners of the square and insert the hinge pieces.

Locking piece

The same principles apply to this locking piece as applied to that in the previous *asa-no-ha*. One end is cut to a 90° point on the 45° jig, and the other end is trimmed to an approximate 112° point on the 56° jig so that it locks the hinges and the pattern in snugly. As in the previous *asa-no-ha*, the 17.9 mm length in the diagram is only a guide, albeit a very accurate guide.

Summary

The only difference between this method and the previous method is the different angles in the hinges and locking piece; the finished *asa-no-ha* is largely indistinguishable from the previous *asa-no-ha*. I prefer the other method because it requires fewer jigs and tends to be faster.

I've included this type here, though, to give you an additional option, and to highlight the fact that exactly the same pattern can be made with slight variations in angles. This will become even more apparent when I cover some of the more complex patterns in subsequent books.

Photograph 160 Type 2 hinges / locking piece relationship

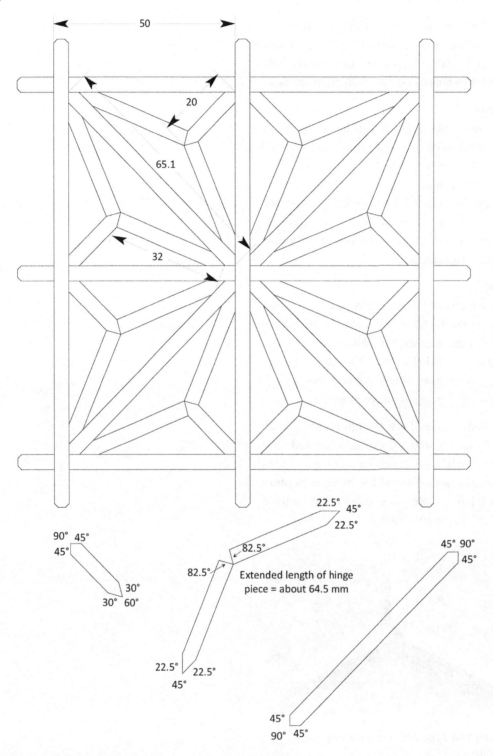

Diagram 124 Ori-mage method

The *ori-mage* method is one in which the hinge piece is cut in the center with a fine-toothed saw so that less than a paper width of timber fiber is left, then bent to house the locking piece, as shown in Diagram 124. This is a strong joint and is the simplest of the three methods, and once you become used to making the fine cuts required, it is also the fastest, although more so in the diamond *jigumi* than in the square *jigumi*.

Kumiko *shokunin* in Japan mostly use a special *kebiki* (marking gauge) to cut several hinges at the same time with a single stroke, but this is normally done with thinner material than the 4.0 mm kumiko we're working with here.

The difficult aspect of this method is cutting the hinge so that the correct thickness of wood fiber remains — too thin and it will break apart, too thick and the piece won't bend cleanly and will look very untidy. And obviously there's always the problem of cutting too much and cutting all the way through. For this reason it's always wise to have a large number of spare pieces.

Ori-mage jigs

The *ori-mage* method of cutting *asa-no-ha* requires a few additional jigs, detailed below.

30° jig

The 30° jig is the same design as the 45° and 22.5° jigs detailed earlier, and is used to trim one end of the locking piece.

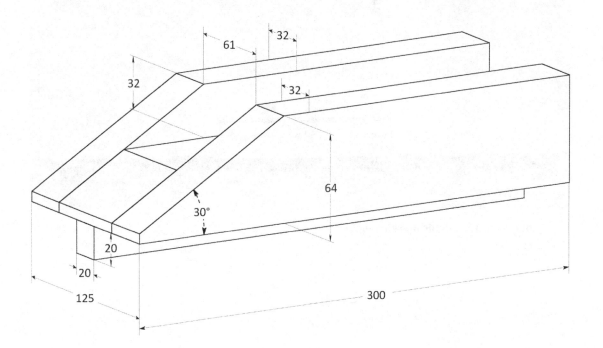

Diagram 125 30° jig

153

Marking jig

I've seen a few different contraptions for cutting these hinge pieces, and there are highly efficient ways of doing this with the appropriate tools, but these are not readily available outside of Japan. Without these tools, I've found the easiest and fastest method is using a very simple marking jig, cutting jig and a desk lamp.

The marking jig is a very simple design consisting of two short pieces of spare kumiko tacked on to a piece of hardwood or MDF. The interval between them is the exact length of the hinge piece fully extended. A third piece of spare kumiko is cut to the hinge piece length and marked across exactly in the center with a marking knife. This piece is then secured between the two other pieces.

The cutting jig is even simpler — a piece of wood with three nails and white tape — and is shown in the text.

Photograph 161 Simple marking jig

Base kumiko (jigumi)

The *jigumi* is exactly the same as the one used in the two previous *asa-no-ha*.

Diagonal pieces

Since the *jigumi* is the same, the diagonal pieces are also the same as in the two previous *asa-no-ha*.

Hinge pieces

Trim the hinge pieces in the 22.5° jig to the required length (64.5 mm) and place in the marking jig.

Photograph 162 Place hinge piece in marking jig

Extend the mark on the reference piece secured in the jig to the hinge piece using a small square and a sharp marking knife. This mark should be in the exact center of the hinge piece.

Photograph 163 Extend the mark

Place the marked hinge piece on the cutting jig, and position a desk lamp so that the light is low and just to the right of the cutting jig.

Photograph 164 Place marked hinge piece on cutting jig

The next part is the key to cutting the hinge, and why there is no need to attach anything to the saw or devise some complex jig to help you cut to the required depth.

Adjust the lamp so that the cutting edge of the saw blade casts a shadow to the left of the cut. The light should be positioned so that when you rest the saw teeth across the hinge piece the shadow of the teeth is blurry, but as you start cutting the shadow becomes sharper. White tape helps make the shadow clearer.

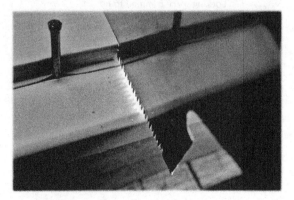

Photograph 165 Saw blade casts a shadow

Work out through trial and error what degree of sharpness the shadow has to be before the hinge has been cut sufficiently, adjusting the light as necessary. This should only take one or two test cuts.

Provided the jig isn't moved and the hinge is placed in the same position every time, this degree of sharpness for the ideal hinge is a constant value, and you very quickly get a feel for how sharp or blurry the shadow is and how much pressure you need to place on the saw as you cut. With practice, this becomes very quick, and on a bad day, with this method I generally expect an 80–90% usable rate for the hinges.

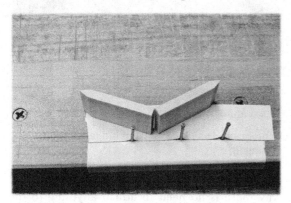

Photograph 166 Cleanly cut hinge piece

Unfortunately, this is not the end of our work on the hinge. The cut you made has left the ends at 90°, but as you can see in the dimensional diagram (Diagram 124), this has to be 82.5° for the locking piece to fit cleanly. If it is left at 90°, the fit is very untidy, and unacceptable, as can be seen in the following diagram.

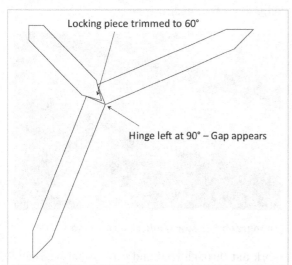

Diagram 126 Gap at bottom of joint

The joint will fit snugly if the end of the locking piece is trimmed at 45° (on the 22.5° jig), but this method is just as untidy.

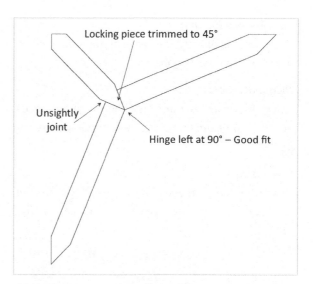

Diagram 127 Unsightly fit on sides

Trimming the end of the locking piece at 45° and reducing the locking piece *mitsuke* so that it fits into the opening leaves a very unbalanced pattern, so the only real option is to adjust the opening of the hinge so that it properly accepts the locking piece.

Therefore, with a very sharp chisel, shave a thin shaving from each side of the hinge opening so that it's closer to the 82.5° than the 90°. Obviously there's no way of measuring this angle, so it's all by feel and judgment. A slight dab of water on the hinge opening to soften the wood will help if the hinges tend to break as you're trimming them with the chisel.

Photograph 167 Trim the hinge opening

Insert the hinge pieces so they fit tightly into the corners formed by the four diagonal pieces.

Photograph 168 Insert hinge pieces

Locking piece

Trim one end of the locking piece in the 30° jig so the end comes to a 60° point. This end fits into the hinge. Trim the other end on the 45° jig so it comes to a 90° point; this end fits into the corner. Test fit and continue trimming the 90° end until it fits with enough tension to close all the joints and hold the hinge piece firmly in place.

Diagram 124 shows a length of 20 mm for the locking piece, but expect the actual length to vary by up to 0.5 mm either way. This variation is because of the minor differences in the overall length of the hinge piece, and marking and cutting, so you will need to test and trim each locking piece to fit.

Photograph 169 Trim and insert locking piece

You can add a dab of glue to the corner and the inside of the hinge if you prefer. Continue with this process until all parts of the *asa-no-ha* have been completed.

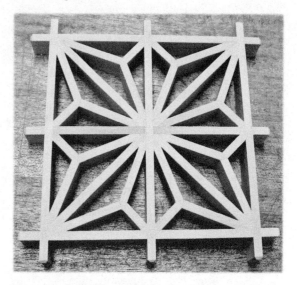

Photograph 170 Completed *asa-no-ha*

Summary

The need for extra work on the hinge opening is the major disadvantage of this method. It's the way I initially learned, and with practice it does become much less of a burden, but it still adds to the time taken to make the *asa-no-ha*, and any time gained is perhaps lost in this additional step. Nonetheless, it is still a very fast and efficient way of cutting the *asa-no-ha*.

Jaguchi

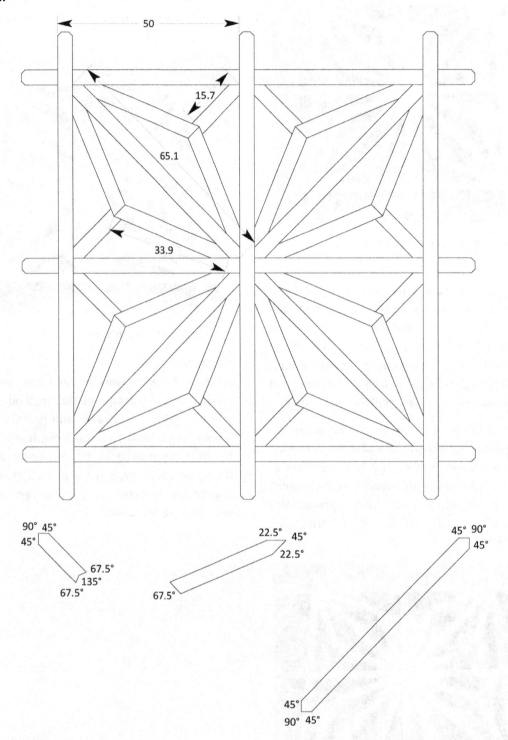

Diagram 128 *Jaguchi* method

The *jaguchi* method is one in which an opening in the end of the locking piece houses the two hinge pieces as shown in the diagram. This is the same *jaguchi* term we use for the ends of the rails where they join the stiles.

This method provides the strongest joint of the different methods, but it is also the most time-consuming, and is not used very often in the *asa-no-ha*. It also requires a special *kebiki* (as shown in the photograph).

There is a special jig for making the *jaguchi* cut, but it's quite complex, and at this stage the other methods are preferable. This jig will be required and explained in the next book where we'll tackle some fairly complicated patterns that have the *jaguchi* joint.

Here, though, I'll explain this method of cutting the *asa-no-ha* purely for information.

As can be seen in the diagram, the hinge pieces are trimmed straight across at 67.5°, and the locking piece has an opening of 135°.

Base kumiko (jigumi)
The *jigumi* is exactly the same as the one used in the other *asa-no-ha*.

Diagonal pieces
Since the *jigumi* is the same, the diagonal pieces are also the same as in the other *asa-no-ha* methods.

Hinge pieces
The hinge pieces are very straightforward. One end is cut to a 45° point on the 22.5° jig, as in the other methods, while the hinge mating end is cut at 67.5° on the 67.5° jig.

Locking piece
The end that fits into the corner is cut at 90° (45° jig) as in the other methods, while the end that joins with the hinges requires the *jaguchi* cut.

The most efficient way of making this cut is with a *kebiki* (a special marking/cutting gauge) and a base jig set at the required angle (in this case 67.5°) and squared off at 90° to that angle, as shown in the following photograph.

Photograph 171 *Kebiki* and jig for making the *jaguchi* cut

The *kebiki* is held firmly against the end, and drawn across the kumiko several times.

Photograph 172 The *kebiki* is held firmly against the end

This continues until the cut reaches about halfway down.

Photograph 173 Cut down to half the thickness

The kumiko are flipped over and cut on the other side to create the *jaguchi* joint.

Photograph 174 Cut the other side to make the *jaguchi*

The kumiko are then cut to rough length at the opposite end, and trimmed to fit in the 45° jig. For this I use my 45° *ha-ganna*, which is explained on Pages 133–134.

Photograph 175 Trim and insert the locking piece

This process is continued until all parts of the *asa-no-ha* have been completed.

Photograph 176 Completed *asa-no-ha*

Summary
Although this method provides the strongest joint, it is also the most time-consuming. The joints in the other methods provide more than adequate strength, so the need for the *jaguchi* in the *asa-no-ha* is debatable. It will, however, be essential for several of the other joints in some of the interesting and complex patterns we tackle in subsequent books.

Asa-no-ha examples

The following are a few examples of how the square *asa-no-ha* can be applied.

Photograph 177 A top and bottom border highlighting and framing a more complex pattern

Photograph 179 A central band

Photograph 178 A subtle central feature

Photograph 180 A dominant central feature

AFTERWORD

Making the decision

In early 2006 Mariko and I started thinking that we needed a change in direction in our work. We had been working as free-lance Japanese-English translators for the best part of 20 years, and huddled over a computer for 10–12 hours a day had gradually lost its appeal and excitement.

Woodworking had become an increasingly serious hobby for me over the preceding years, and with Mariko's understanding and blessing, this was the direction the next phase of our life together would take.

Shoji seemed to be the natural choice — it is a traditional Japanese craft with its own unique beauty, it requires a high level of skill and patience, and shoji itself is an inherent part of Japanese culture and the Japanese psyche.

But to do justice to the tradition of shoji, I wanted the formal training that could give me the foundations for adapting shoji and kumiko craftwork to suit the woodworking methods and tools we have available in the West.

I eventually came across the website of Shokugei Gakuin (Toyama International College of Craft and Arts). The College program and philosophy seemed perfect, and a visit to the College in mid 2006 reinforced this view.

An exchange of emails followed, and I was set to start with the March 2008 intake.

Shokugei Gakuin is in picturesque Toyama Prefecture, on the Japan Sea side of Japan's main island of Honshu. It's located in a natural setting in the foothills of the Tateyama mountains, and a range of natural wildlife, including monkeys, deer and *tanuki* are regular visitors.

The College was founded in 1996 through the vision of the current Board of Directors Chairman, Mr. Minoru Inaba, one of life's true gentlemen. It is divided into the construction/building course, which is further classified into carpentry, furniture, and *tategu*, and the gardening and landscape course.

The *shokunin* spirit is central to the College's teaching philosophy, and traditional hand skills and techniques are at the heart of all training. Students in the normal two-year intake, both in the construction and gardening courses, spend most of their practical training in the first six months under the watchful eye of the senior *tōryō* (master carpenter) learning how to sharpen and use *kanna* and chisels. At the end of this six months the students' skill in hand-tool use and maintenance is very advanced indeed.

Because of my previous woodworking experience, I was placed directly into the postgraduate course in *tategu*, under my instructor, Isao Sawada Sensei, a highly skilled second-generation *tategushi*. It was under his guidance that I was able to develop the foundations in shoji that would give me the confidence and knowledge to take this to a different level and tackle *kumiko-zaiku*.

I was the first foreigner to complete a full course at the College, although other foreigners have completed shorter courses designed for their specific needs. All instruction at the College is in Japanese.

Professionally, the course was everything I had hoped it would be. To be trained by and associate with the top *shokunin* in their field was a unique experience that has been of immeasurable value. But what I gained from the College goes well beyond mere *kanna*, saws and chisels: Sawada Sensei and the other instructors taught me what it means to be a *shokunin*, and the significance and importance of the *shokunin* spirit.

The Shokugei Gakuin website can be found at http://shokugei.ac.jp. The website is in Japanese, but an English pamphlet outlining the College's curriculum and philosophy can be viewed at http://shokugei.ac.jp/english.pdf.

In compiling the book

One of the widely published academic instructors at Shokugei Gakuin — Sachio Ueno Sensei — first planted the thought of a book on shoji in my mind toward the end of my studies at the College.

After completing the course, I initially set myself a five-year time-frame to start writing. The first few years would be spent on researching and building up my repertoire of kumiko patterns, then once I had completed arguably the most difficult of all the kumiko patterns — *ami-mono* — I would start on the book.

The *ami-mono* pattern is in the shape of a fishing net (*ami* is Japanese for net). Within the *ami-mono* pattern there are several variations, including a net being cast, a net being hauled from the water, and a net hung out to dry. The pattern's difficulty is that each cut must be made at a different angle and different interval to achieve a smooth shape. These angles, however, are not set. They have to be calculated depending on size, shape, expanse and flow of the net, and various other factors. There are also different methods of calculation depending on the desired relationship between the arrangement of the different kumiko "threads" within the net. And the larger the pattern, the more cuts and calculations that are required.

Unfortunately, because of the time needed to calculate, cut and assemble this pattern, it is not seen as much these days as it was in the past, and there is a risk that over the next couple of generations of kumiko *shokunin*, the skill to make this pattern by hand could be lost.

With Mariko's encouragement, I decided to bring forward my timetable. The *ami-mono* pattern could wait for a subsequent book in which I would document and share my first attempt at this pattern, including mistakes and lessons learned.

What should the book contain? This was obviously the first aspect I had to have clear in my mind before I could even begin to build the framework of the book. I could have adopted the shotgun approach and include scatterings of bits and pieces of shoji designs and patterns, but this lack of a structured approach would be of only very limited value. So I decided to structure the book largely based on the way I learned shoji and kumiko at Shokugei Gakuin — from the basics.

I very quickly realized that I would need probably three books to realistically reach my ultimate goal — detailed description and instruction on the *ami-mono* pattern.

This is the first book, and it covers exactly what the title describes: the basics of shoji and kumiko design. Being able to make the much more complex kumiko patterns, some of which I feature on my website, requires a solid foundation in making shoji, so I encourage you to go through the shoji and patterns, including the various exercises, in this book as a step-by-step learning program. This will give you good grounding for the more difficult designs.

Subsequent books will focus mainly on kumiko patterns and arrangements, each slightly more complex or difficult than the pattern before, and how they fit into the overall shoji design.

References

The vast majority of the information in this book is based on instruction I received at Shokugei Gakuin from Sawada Sensei.

Although not a formal bibliography as such, the following is a list of the books I referred to during the course of writing the different sections:

(1) *Shokugei Kenchiku Jisshū Kyōkasho*, 2008, Shokugei Gakuin (This is the textbook used at the College, and the individual sections were written by the respective instructors.)

(2) *Tedōgu de no Kakō*, Tadashi Kakitani (This is a booklet written by Shokugei Gakuin's furniture instructor, Kakitani Sensei, and is one of the best and most comprehensive references on *kanna* and chisels I've seen.)

(3)   *Tategu Seisaku Kyōhon Vol. 1, 2 and 3*, 2002, Zenkoku Tategu Sōgō Rengō-Kai (First published in 1984, these three volumes form the "bible" of *tategu*.)

(4)   *Tategu Hinagata Zuan Zenshū Vol. 5*, 1954, Tategu Kōgei Kenkyū-Kai (This is one of six outstanding volumes dealing with kumiko patterns; they contain very little information about how to make the patterns, but the diagrams are invaluable for analyzing how they are structured.)

(5)   *Mokusei Tategu Design Zukan*, 2000, Mokusei Tategu Kenkyū-Kai et.al (A large and very comprehensive book on various aspects of *tategu*, including history.)

(6)   *Mokuzō no Shōsai, Vol. 4 Tategu Zōsaku*, 2003, Shōkoku-sha (A very good book on *tategu* showing detailed drawings of many different designs.)

(7)   *Zu de Wakaru Daiku Dōgu*, 2005, Rikō Gakusha (An excellent book by Isota Nagao showing detailed drawings of many Japanese hand tools.)

(8)   *Kanna Daizen*, 2009, Seibundo Shinkosha (This relatively newly published book contains almost everything there is to know about *kanna*.)

Thank you for purchasing this book, and I hope you find it of some value. Good luck with your endeavors, and if you have any queries or comments, please feel free to contact me through my website at http://kskdesign.com.au.

Des King
December 2011

APPENDIX

Glossary

The following is a list of the Japanese terms I've used in this book, and their English equivalent, or the location in the book where their meaning is explained.

Akari-shōji	Old term for present-day shoji
Aragumi-shōji (also *arama-shōji*)	Type of kumiko arrangement (Page 54)
Ara-shikō	Rough planing
Asa-no-ha	Kumiko pattern (Page 142)
Ashi	Flat sides of the blade *ura* (Page 10)
Atama	Top of the *kanna* blade (Page 10)
Beta-ura	The shape of the *ura* on a chisel (Page 42)
Bu	Old unit of measurement — about 3.03 mm. Ten *bu* make one *sun* (refer to *Shaku* below). (See Page 79)
Chū-shikō	Intermediate planing
Dai	Wooden block housing the blade and chip-breaker in a *kanna* (Page 6)
Dai-gashira	"Front" of the *kanna*, but would equate to the back of a Western plane (Page 7)
Dai-jiri	"Back" of the *kanna*, but would equate to the front of a Western plane (Page 7)
Dai-kanna	Wooden-bodied *kanna* (Page 5)
Dai-koba / koba	Side surface of the *kanna* (Page 7)
Dainaoshi kanna	*Kanna* for conditioning *kanna* sole (Page 17)
Dai-shitaba / shitaba	*Kanna* sole (Page 7)
Dai-uwaba / uwaba	Top surface of the *kanna* (Page 7)
Dōzuki	Japanese saw with a firm metal spine to provide stiffness to the blade
Ennuki-shōji	Small set of shoji above shoji doors, traditionally through which smoke from an internal cooking fire and the like could escape (Photograph Page 48)

Fukiyose-shōji	Shoji in which the kumiko are arranged in groups (Photograph Page 48; Page 54)
Fusuma	Sliding doors and room dividers covered with thick opaque paper
Fusuma-shōji	*Fusuma*
Futae kaku-tsunagi	Kumiko pattern (Page 136)
Gakuiri-shōji	Shoji that contain a glass frame (Page 55)
Genkan	Entrance to a Japanese house
Genkotsu	Type of joinery connecting hinge and locking pieces (Page 142)
Gennō	Japanese hammer (Page 25)
Hagane	Thin layer of hard steel forming the cutting edge on a laminated *kanna* blade or chisel (Page 9)
Ha-ganna	Highly specialized *kanna* used in *kumiko-zaiku* (Page 133)
Ha-guchi	*Kanna* mouth (Page 8)
Hake	Generic term for a brush.
Ha-saki	Blade cutting edge (Page 11)
Hatagane	Clamp
Hikichigai-nekoma	Type of *nekoma-shōji* (Page 56)
Hikiwake-nekoma	Type of *nekoma-shōji* (Page 56)
Hikōki-kanna	Type of *kanna* used in *tategu* (Page 8)
Hinoki	Japanese cypress
Hira-ganna	Japanese smoothing plane (Page 14)
Honshige-shōji	Kumiko arrangement with a large number of vertical and horizontal kumiko (Page 54)
Ito-ura	A thinly formed *uraba* – this is the ideal *ura* shape (Page 42)
Izutsu-tsunagi	Kumiko pattern (Page 129)
Jaguchi	(1) 45° projection from the ends of rails (see Page 72), also called *umanori*. (2) Type of joinery connecting hinge and locking pieces (Page 158)

Jigane	Thick layer of soft metal on a laminated *kanna* blade or chisel (Page 9)
Jigumi	Base kumiko structure that houses the intricate kumiko patterns (Page 129)
Jikagarasu-shōji	Shoji containing a large glass frame (Page 56).
Jō-shikō (kanna) / shiage-kanna	Finish planing (finish plane)
Kaesaki	Boundary between the *hagane* and *jigane* on a laminated *kanna* blade (Page 10)
Kagami	Angled face opposite *omote-najimi*
Kakumen-ganna	Chamfer plane with adjustable fence (Page 23)
Kamoi	Head jamb
Kanna	Japanese hand-plane
Karakami	Patterned paper introduced from China during the Heian Period
Karakami-shōji	Old term for present-day *fusuma*
Kasumi-gumi shōji	Kumiko pattern in which thinner kumiko convey the feeling of mist enveloping the shoji (Page 100)
Kata	Shoulders of the *kanna* blade (Page 10)
Katabiki-nekoma	Type of *nekoma-shōji* (Page 56)
Kawari-gumi shōji	Shoji containing a variation of the standard shoji pattern, or a pattern that alternates between the left and right sides of the shoji (Page 117)
Kebiki	Generic term for Japanese marking gauge
Keyaki	Zelkova
Kichō	Hanging cloth screen
Kireba	Bevel (both blade and chip-breaker) (Page 11)
Kiri	Paulownia
Kiri-kaeshi	Kumiko pattern in which the kumiko are joined in a weave pattern (Page 90)
Kiwa-ganna	Rebate planes (Page 19)
Kōana	Top opening in *kanna* (Page 7)

Ko-ganna	Small *kanna*. Generally *kanna* 48 mm and smaller are referred to as *ko-ganna*, but this is not a hard and fast rule.
Koppa-gaeshi	Bottom part of the *kagami* on a *kanna dai* (Page 7)
Koshidaka-shōji	*Koshitsuki-shōji* with a high hip-board (Page 54)
Koshitsuki-shōji	Shoji with a hip-board (Page 56)
Ko-shōji	Small moveable shoji frame within the overall shoji
Kōzu	A particularly attractive kumiko pattern consisting of many internal miter joints.
Kumiko	Thin pieces of wood forming the lattice in shoji.
Kumiko shokunin	*Shokunin* who specialize in making highly intricate kumiko patterns
Kumiko-zaiku	The art of making highly intricate patterns with kumiko
Maru-zan	Type of top rail (Page 89)
Masugumi-shōji	Kumiko arrangement in which the kumiko form squares (Page 54)
Men-jiri / Men-ochi	Type of cross-piece joinery in which both pieces are chamfered, and one piece is set below the chamfer line of the other (Page 90)
Men-tori kanna	Molding planes (Page 23)
Mikomi	Sides of the kumiko (Page 52)
Mimi	(1) On a blade — angled ends of the cutting edge (Page 10) (2) On a chip-breaker — bent top corners to apply tension to the blade (Page 11)
Mitsuke	Front of the kumiko (Page 52)
Mizugoshi-shōji	Standard form of shoji structure (Page 54)
Moya	Large open-spaced room featured in the *shinden-zukuri* architectural style.
Nageshi-zan	Type of top rail (Page 89)
Nekoma-shōji	Shoji containing *ko-shōji* that move horizontally in grooves (Page 55)
Nokogiri	Japanese saw
Ōgakuiri-shōji	See *Jikagarasu-shōji* above
Ōire nomi	Japanese butt chisels

Omote (*senaka / kō*)	Front of the *kanna* blade (Page 10)
Omote-najimi (*senaka-najimi*)	Part of *dai* that supports the blade (Page 7)
Ori-mage	Type of joinery connecting hinge and locking pieces (Page 152)
Osae-bō	Pressure pin in *kanna* to apply tension to the blade and chip-breaker (Page 8)
Osae-mizo	Side groove in *kanna* (Page 8)
Ranma	Transom window, often featuring very elaborate kumiko patterns or carvings
Rin	Old unit of measurement — about 0.303 mm. Ten *rin* make one *bu* (refer to *Shaku* below). (See Page 79)
Ryōba	Japanese saw with teeth set for cross-cut on one side and rip-cut on the other
Shaku	Old Japanese unit of measurement — about 303 mm. This form of measurement was officially discontinued in 1966 but is still used in traditional carpentry, *tategu*, and by some furniture-makers. (See Page 79)
Shikii	Threshold
Shinden-zukuri	Architectural style introduced during the Heian Period (794–1185)
Shoin-shōji	Often very elaborate shoji associated with the *shoin-zukuri* style
Shoin-zukuri	Important and influential architectural style that became firmly established during the Momoyama Period (1573–1603)
Shoji / *shōji*	Generic term for doors, windows and room dividers with translucent paper-backed lattice panel within a frame.
Shokunin	Craftsmen and artisans; the term *shokunin* in Japan carries with it a heightened social obligation above that normally associated with craftsmen in the West.
Sugi	Japanese cedar
Sun	Old unit of measurement — about 30.3 mm. Ten *sun* make one *shaku* (refer to *Shaku* above). (See Page 79)
Sokosarai nomi	Japanese chisel designed to clean waste from the bottom of mortises (also called *sokozarai nomi*)

Suriage-shōji	Type of shoji structure with a small shoji frame that can be raised and lowered (Page 56). Other common names include *yukimi-shōji*, *suriage-nekoma*, and *ōsaka-nekoma*.
Tategakuiri-shōji	Shoji containing a rectangular glass frame with a vertical orientation (Page 56)
Tategu	Collective and generic term covering all internal and external doors and windows.
Tategumi-shōji	Vertically oriented kumiko arrangement (Page 54)
Tateguya / tategushi	Craftsmen or businesses that make and install *tategu*
Tateshige-shōji	More pronounced vertically oriented kumiko arrangement with a large number of vertical kumiko (Page 54)
Tokonoma	Alcove in traditional Japanese homes for displaying flowers, scrolls or ornaments
Tōryō	Master carpenter
Tsuitate	Partitioning screen (Page 135)
Tsukeko	Internal frame between the kumiko and mainframe (Page 51). For the different types in common use see Page 84.
Tsuki-kanna	Name for *kanna* introduced from China (Page 5)
Tsutsumi	Small extension from the bottom of the *omote-najimi* (Page 8)
Ura	Back of the blade (Page 10)
Uraba	Flat area forming one side of the cutting edge (Page 10)
Ura-dashi	Tapping out a blade or chip-breaker (Page 38)
Uragane	Chip-breaker
Uragire	Condition of the *ura* after regular sharpening when the *uraba* vanishes and the *urasuki* reaches the cutting edge (Page 38)
Ura-oshi	Flattening the back of a blade or chip-breaker (Page 26)
Urasuki	Hollow in a laminated *kanna* blade (Page 10)
Usu-zan	Type of top rail (Page 89)
Washi	Japanese hand-made paper

Yae kaku-tsunagi	Kumiko pattern based on the *futae kaku-tsunagi* but more complex (Page 138)
Yanagi-shōji	"Willow shoji" — another name for *tateshige-shōji*
Yari-ganna	Early Japanese plane shaped like a spear (Page 5)
Yokogakuiri-shōji	Shoji containing a rectangular glass frame with a horizontal orientation (Page 56)
Yokogumi-shōji	Horizontally oriented kumiko arrangement (Page 54)
Yokoshige-shōji	More pronounced horizontally oriented kumiko arrangement containing a large number of horizontal kumiko (Page 54)
Yukimi-shōji	"Snow-viewing shoji" — see *Suriage-shōji* above.

INDEX

Made in the USA
Las Vegas, NV
10 July 2024

92120900R00103